MORE

THE REDISCOVERY OF AMERICAN COMMON SENSE

R.Q. Armington and William D. Ellis

REGNERY GATEWAY • CHICAGO

Illustrations by Phil Kantz from drawings by Glenn Pierce

Library of Congress Cataloging in Publication Data

Armington, Raymond Q., 1907–
  More: the rediscovery of American common sense.

  Bibliography: p.
  Includes index.
  1. Liberty. 2. Laissez-faire. 3. United States—
Politics and government. I. Ellis, William Donohue.
II. Title.
JC585.A67 1984 320.5'12 84-42679
ISBN 0-89526-605-9

Manufactured in the United States of America

Published by Regnery Gateway, Inc.
360 West Superior Street
Chicago, Illinois 60610

To a new generation,
for the better care and
handling of America...
in memory of
Charles R. "Chuck" Armington

AUTHORS' NOTE:

The most concise statement of the goal of the American working man was roared without benefit of microphone across an audience of hundreds by labor lion Samuel Gompers—"More!"

Later heard by thousands, it clearly meant more dollars.

Today the goal is the same, but now the route to *more*...is to raise the value of those dollars.

And surprisingly that gets down to the common sense of increasing personal freedom.

Raymond Q. Armington
and
William D. Ellis

ACKNOWLEDGING...

the help of Dr. Russell Kirk, who, despite his own severe work schedule, reviewed the manuscript in progress several times, giving the benefit of his judgment and encyclopedic knowledge; the suggestion of John Shaw, recommending a pivotal reference work, *The Lincoln Encyclopedia* by Archer H. Shaw; the attention of Pauline Fanslow to the manuscript throughout several drafts; the work of previous investigators of these subjects, listed as suggested reading at the end of this book; the literary services of Bob Oskam, agent.

R.Q.A.
W.D.E.

CONTENTS

FOREWORD

by Russell Kirk

This slim book is concerned with more freedom and more money. Taking Tom Paine and Abraham Lincoln for their exemplars, the authors hope that their lively chapters may persuade many Americans to work intelligently for political and economic renewal.

What constricts the American nation nowadays, they tell us, is what Alexis de Tocqueville termed "democratic despotism." As early as the 1830s, de Tocqueville perceived that democratic nations in general tend to bind themselves with invisible chains.

"I seek to trace the novel features under which despotism may appear in the world," de Tocqueville wrote. *"The first thing that strikes the observation is an innumerable multitude of men, all equal and all alike, incessantly endeavoring to procure the petty and paltry pleasures with which they glut their lives. Each of them, living apart, is as a stranger to all the rest; his children and his private friends constitute to him the whole of mankind. . . .*

"Above this race of men stands an immense and tutelary power, which takes upon itself alone to secure their gratifications and to watch over their fate. That power is absolute, minute, regular, provident, and mild. It would be like the authority of a parent if, like that authority, its object was to prepare men for manhood; but it seeks, on the contrary, to keep them in perpetual childhood; it is well content that the people should rejoice, provided that they think of nothing but rejoicing. For their happiness such a government willingly labors, but it chooses to be the sole agent and the only arbiter of their necessities, facilitates their pleasures, manages their principal concerns, directs their industry, regulates the descent of property, and subdivides their inheritances; what remains, but to spare them all the care of thinking and all the trouble of living?

"Thus it every day renders the exercise of the free agency of man less useful and less frequent; it circumscribes the will within a narrower range and gradually robs a man of all the uses of himself. The principle of equality has prepared men for these things; it has predisposed them to endure them and often to look on them as benefits."

Such is the character of democratic despotism, far more advanced now in America than it was a century and a half ago. Mr. Armington and Mr. Ellis endeavor to wake the American people to their present sunken condition—and to offer recommendations for emancipation.

The United States stands in no present danger of a military dictator or the rule of fanatic ideologues. Rather, increasingly the country is weighed down by bureaucratic fussiness, burdensome taxation, and mediocrity of spirit. Individual aspiration is discouraged; dullness becomes public policy. Only concerned measures of protest and reinvigoration can arrest this drift into general decadence.

Armington and Ellis ask for something more than leveling complacency, which would keep us all in perpetual childhood. They seek more independence of character, more public spirit, more money for those who work for it—and less direction by the political power at Washington. They emphasize especially the need for reduction of public expenditures and for a sound currency—objectives closely related, for excessive expenditure requires either excessive taxation or perilous inflation of the currency—or both simultaneously. Thus productive capital is reduced, more and more citizens become dependent upon the government's largesse, and true freedom is diminished. A servile economy produces political and personal servility.

The authors' method for rousing the great sleepy public is the true narration. The greater part of this book consists of illustrative anecdotes extracted from our newspapers and magazines. How perceptive these episodes are, and how alarming! The best way to make a telling point always has been the practical illustration; Armington and Ellis succeed in piecing together, from grim or comical fragments, a picture of the United States slothfully and unconsciously sinking into democratic despotism. From these vignettes of what has been done to our neighbors, we learn what may be done to us, and soon. Education, manufacturing, agriculture, our pocketbooks, our private lives—nothing is exempt from the heavy hand of officialdom.

This is no new experience, historically considered. The Roman system sank to its ruin under the weight of taxation and debased coinage. The mercantile and manufacturing classes were crushed; the state itself became the major manufacturer, presently; the urban population lived at public expense—until the public revenues no longer could be collected. And as the Roman economy declined, the remnants of political liberty trickled away, with much of the population reduced to serfdom. Great civilizations do come to an end, chiefly for lack of imagination and vigor.

Presumably most Americans nowadays fancy that American creature comforts and American liberties will continue undiminished, no matter what is done in Washington and no matter how little any citizen may contribute to the public good. Armington and Ellis know otherwise. It is only through vigorous public action that a decline of American prosperity and of civic freedom may be averted. In the eighth chapter of this little book, practical means are outlined by which the citizen of the American Republic can affect public policies.

In the Carboniferous Epoch we were promised abundance for all,
By robbing selected Peter to pay for collective Paul;
But, though we had plenty of money, there was nothing our money could
*   buy,*
And the Gods of the Copybook Headings said: "If you don't work you
*   die."*

So Rudyard Kipling wrote in 1917. Mr. Armington and Mr. Ellis are telling us something very similar in 1984. Liberty and prosperity are bought with a price. And the later the hour, the higher that price.

1

MORE PROSPERITY— LESS GOVERNMENT

A CASE OF THE UNITED STATES

VS.

JOE PINGA ET AL.

Freedom is a Dollar?

XENIA, OHIO. Widower C. J. Meiggs held a garage sale. The apartment owner said he could use his space in the apartment garage for that.

Meiggs sold off a 1 ½ h.p. garden tractor with attachments, a post hole digger, a small bench saw, and about sixty shop and garden tools.

His face was work lined and his knuckles big with arthritis, but his spirit was young.

Like a lot of unsung heroes, Clover Meiggs had worked steadily all his life at a job he didn't hate but didn't love either. What kept him going was family expenses... plus a dream.

On retirement, he would buy ten acres, cultivate some specialized small acreage items to sell on a stand out front... blueberries, rhubarb, mint... odd items. Then, in the winter he would refinish antique furniture for sale. Over the years he collected a few tools. So he was ready.

Meiggs had not made the moves the cool ones had made.

Hadn't invested in securities (except for war bonds) nor bought a condo on credit. He knew he probably should have; had talked about it with Eleanor. But they felt they didn't know enough about these things, and they feared debt.

So they decided, despite inflation, they would just work hard, educate the two boys and the girl, and save what they could. Then, on retirement, they would buy the ten acres. They had spotted the place; it had a cabin and a garage, town water, and a good price.

They had put $46,000 by over the years. But the daughter turned out to be a brilliant musician. Graduate school costs ran five figures. Then Eleanor went into the hospital. Expenses went beyond Meiggs' coverage.

Even so, after Eleanor was gone, Meiggs went out to talk again to the owner of the land with the cabin on it.

Times had changed. $97,500! "Inflation, Clover. I'm sorry."

Meiggs looked around for six months.

What he finally found was a home that would take his entire savings and guarantee him a room for life.

No room for his tools. Hence a garage sale.

Clover Meiggs lost his liberty.

So did we all.

Meiggs' loss of personal freedom was locked to the unsoundness of his money. The unsoundness of his money is locked to the unsoundness of his government. And that gets back to us. We want more value in our dollar. How can we get that? How can we keep it?

The once sound American dollar has been whittled down in value since 1934 to where it now buys a dime's worth. That kind of loss of value robs us of the liberty to plan our lives.

To avoid disaster, this value erosion must be stopped and gradually reversed. With high productivity, the soundness of the dollar can gradually be restored, along with the freedom. Strong incentives for both individual initiative and individual concern for the well-being of others can accomplish this, provided we reduce the load of big government to a bare minimum.

This can be done...with common sense.

This volume, referring back to the experiences of proven leaders, is a prescription for restoring our freedom. In 1775

Thomas Paine wrote his best-selling pamphlet, "Common Sense," a piercing message urging American independence. This same common sense is needed today. Introducing his pamphlet, Paine wrote:

Perhaps the sentiments contained in the following pages, are not yet sufficiently fashionable to procure them general favor; a long habit of not thinking a thing wrong, gives it a superficial appearance of being right, and raises at first a formidable outcry in defence of custom. But the tumult soon subsides. Time makes more converts than reason.

. . . a long and violent abuse of power, is generally the Means of calling the right of it in question (and in Matters too which might never have been thought of, had not the Sufferers been aggravated into the inquiry. . .).

It Can't Happen Here?

Power abuse sneaks in too softly to awaken any heroics, sometimes even arriving as a laugh.

DEERFIELD, ILLINOIS. A sign outside the commuter train station of this Chicago suburb as of this writing prohibits commuters kissing spouses goodbye. That bottlenecks traffic. The village government has therefore decreed a "no kissing zone."

Hitting the AP wire, it became a national chuckle.

In the midst of such good fun, who but a clod would note the unsmiling tyranny of a tiny government?

He'd have to be some kind of nut, right?

HUBBARD, IOWA. Another funny story. Iowa girls' high school basketball has different rules, six players, three forwards and three guards, and only two dribbles.

A lot of people worried that good Iowa girl basketball players would be disadvantaged when they went on to college basketball and regular women's rules. The Iowa Civil Rights Commission wanted to mandate that Iowa girls play conventional basketball. Governor Robert Ray, on the other hand, felt schools should be able to play basketball however they want.

But it reached national levels. The federal department of Health, Education, and Welfare (since broken into two departments: Education and Health and Human Services) felt it necessary to study Iowa girls' basketball.

In Arkansas the same issue flared. A federal judge decreed that different rules deprived girls of equal opportunity.

A federal judge in Tennessee ruled against six-girl basketball. A big laugh. Certainly.

Or does it worry anybody that the United States government turns its awesome power on girls' basketball?

CHICAGO. Mike Royko's syndicated column tells about the Government vs. Gwen Noble. Receiving no mail for two weeks, Gwen Noble went to Lake View Branch, U.S. Post Office, and asked the woman at the desk for her mail.

"We aren't general delivery. I can't hand you your mail."

Overhearing this, a nearby male postal employee explained that Mrs. Noble's mail was probably not arriving because of unshoveled sidewalks at her residence. Carriers aren't required to deliver through snow.

Mrs. Noble said the sidewalk was clear enough for her. Would he at least look to see if she had mail. He did so and returned, "Yes."

She was expecting a check. Could she have it?

"No." It had to be delivered.

Mrs. Noble checked with the main post office. Same story.

Hearing this, columnist Mike Royko phoned the supervisor of customer complaints, James Paige. Same story. Royko asked, "If they won't deliver the mail, and she can't pick it up, how does she get it?"

"I guess she is just going to have to clear her street."

Further discussion developed that the sidewalks and street in front of the large apartment building were clean. However, said Mr. Paige, the snow problem is up or down the street from her, endangering the postman's life, "her mail will not be delivered."

Royko asked how the poor woman could get her mail.

"She can get it anytime she can get the city and her landlord to clean up the street."

A funny story about government versus the citizen? Yes. But a little less funny, right?

ALBUQUERQUE, NEW MEXICO. An older couple sitting

in their back yard in the cool of the evening is startled. In the sky a very high intensity light suddenly appears, focuses on them brightly, and advances.

The couple are first frightened, then infuriated. This is the nose spotlight on an Albuquerque police plane on routine patrol. This low-flying police spy plane patrols in the daylight as well. One woman had to stop sunbathing on her roof—the local government plane kept circling above her.

A funny government story? Sort of.

However, in the same town is another government story, less funny. A woman worked many years to be sure her daughter could go to college. Belatedly she learned to her surprise that her high school daughter had been shifted from college preparatory courses to vocational courses. In answer to the parents' questions, the school administrators only referred her to the officials of the federally funded vocational program to which her daughter had been diverted. Their response was that the vocational program was designed by experts who knew what was in the best interests of the daughter.

Government becomes now even less funny.

RICE, VIRGINIA. This is a little crossroads town where the trees meet over the street and business people treated each other as neighbors and friends.

Preston Carrington ran Carrington's Wayside Mobile Home Sales with a pleasant informality. If Allye Payne, a bookkeeper, needed an afternoon off for some shopping, no problem. If Mr. Carrington wanted her to come in some Saturday morning, no problem. In the same way, Lew Martin worked extra time prior to November so he could go deer hunting in the fall. Worked out fine. People liked it that way.

But the U.S. Labor Department did not.

S. Douglas Guthrie is the U.S. Labor Department investigator for eight counties, one of a thousand "compliance officers" in the nation. He drove over from Lynchburg, conscientious and businesslike. Came to Carrington's first thing Monday morning; asked to see the books and talk to employees.

Carrington asked him what it was all about.

"Strictly routine."

"Because I thought it was routine," Carrington explained

later, "shoot, I opened up my books completely."

But never again.

When Mr. Guthrie of the Labor Department finished his examination, Mr. Carrington was startled to find he was in violation of two federal wage-hour guidelines. He paid his workers fixed weekly paychecks regardless if hours worked were over or under. When business was down in winter, Carrington sent his employees home and still paid the regular amount. When business was brisk, his people worked extra time. But Guthrie said Carrington owed them time-and-a-half for that. Same for Lew's extra hours getting ready for his deer hunting trip and Allye Payne's Saturday morning work.

It didn't matter that the employees liked the way things were run here. "The law doesn't recognize an employee's right to waive his rights," Mr. Guthrie explained.

Guthrie said Carrington owed $6,000 back pay to employees and former employees; and so that he could oversee the payment process, he asked Carrington to write the checks immediately in his presence.

Well...the three employees said they didn't want the money, wouldn't accept it. In fact two former employees, who on this basis were owed overtime, owed Mr. Carrington more for loans than Carrington owed them. They were embarrassed.

But on Mr. Guthrie's side was the government.

Mr. Carrington is still in business. "But it's different now. Not so pleasant."

Rice, Virginia, is different now.

MILWAUKEE, WISCONSIN. A group of doctors look around Milwaukee for an empty building to rent close enough to the hospital to house a CAT scanner, but obscure enough to attract little attention.

Doctors generally consider the computerized axial tomograph scanner—the CAT scanner—one of the greatest diagnostic tools. For example, physicians can often tell, quickly enough to help, whether a suddenly paralyzed victim has had a stroke or has a tumor. Speed is crucial in the one case.

The CAT scanner eliminates much dangerous exploratory surgery.

However, big hospital capital acquisitions are controlled by a federal health planning act administered by state and local health planning agencies.

A certificate of need (CON) must be filed. The probability of turn-down has induced doctors to band together to buy scanners as private individuals and set them up off hospital grounds to avoid the federal bureacracy.

The Milwaukee doctors have found an empty fast-food building. However, Wisconsin, along with other states who call these "fugitive scanners," want to forbid this practice.

CAT scanners in certain towns may not be sound economics, but when government is the one to make that decision, then the laugh is gone out of the joke.

WEST WARWICK, RHODE ISLAND. Joe Pinga had been away from his bakery. He returned to find a letter saying that he was charged with violating twelve federal regulations in his bakery—electric plugs with two prongs instead of three, one safety rail four inches too low—things like that. Fine: $90.

Pinga, a second generation patriot, was hurt, "My God, how can I be guilty; I haven't even had a trial."

HINCKLEY TOWNSHIP, OHIO. John Karasek, a man approaching retirement age, farmed fifty-nine acres at 309 Ledge Road, what was left of his father's farm where John was brought up. This working farm, partially supporting Mr. and Mrs. Karasek, was their retirement security.

And then the Karaseks received a shock. The three commissioners of the Medina County metropark system, invoking the right of eminent domain, voted to buy the rear forty-three acres of Karasek's farm, 70 percent of it, leaving him sixteen acres and his barn and buildings, but not enough land for a viable farm. The commissioners took this action in full knowledge that Karasek didn't want to sell.

Karasek fought it; but he had two formidable opponents, his county government and the federal government.

Park District Director Harold Schick explained to the public in print that the main issue with respect to Karasek's land was "the greatest good of *all* people." The land, even if little was done with it, would benefit present and future park users, he explained. Schick also said the Karasek purchase would square up the park holdings nicely. "We've made every effort possible to talk to these people," Schick stated, defending the reasonability of the government action.

Mrs. Karasek, a spunky lady of sixty-five, asked the park administrators, "Why can't you wait until we're deceased to take the land? We don't have children, so we won't care then."

A lot of people chuckle about a government so powerful it can tell us how we should play basketball. But...the Karasek's farm?

HILLSDALE, MICHIGAN. There is an attractive little college here with a lot of character, 1100 students, and a lot of enthusiastic alumni: Hillsdale College. You've probably heard about it for the following reason.

It is independent. It never asked for a cent from the federal government. So it returned blank the "recipient institution" forms sent to it by the government.

However, the federal department of Health, Education and Welfare informed Hillsdale that even if only *one* of its students receives a federal grant, the entire college is considered a "recipient institution," subject to all federal rules, procedures, paperwork, programs, and inspections.

Hillsdale, under leadership of gutsy President George Roche, resisted, but it entered a tough fight. The federal government is now dictator to most major colleges.

When Dartmouth wanted to hire a new dean, it followed federal regulations and advertised in national publications. Deluged with five hundred applications, the university would have had to set up evaluation committees and pay for four long trips across the nation to interview candidates in many cities. They couldn't afford it, so went without.

Colleges that once welcomed federal money now cannot disengage the federal octopus.

The president of Asbury College, Wilmare, Kentucky says, "The careful respect by government for the independence of the educational world is long gone. Noninvolvement has changed to enormous intrusion; respect has changed to control. The extent is frightening."

Part of that extent is thirty-four congressional committees and seventy subcommittees with jurisdiction over 439 laws affecting college education, translated by bureaus into over 1000 pages of regulations.

President Bok of Harvard told his alumni, "The critical issue for the next generation is not Harvard's survival, but its independence from ill-advised government restraint."

Many college presidents now spend one-quarter of their time coping with government control.

Economist Earl Cheit points out that bureaucrats "require the gathering of useless data; they cause long inexplicable delays; they play 'cat and mouse' games over enforcement; they conduct endless reviews."

The bureaucracy at work in education is sometimes funny, like HEW's sexual equality campaign, leading to discontinuance of father-son banquets and boys' choirs. Unfunny are the threatening costs imposed. To develop affirmative action plans at the University of Michigan cost $350,000.

Ohio State University spent $885,000 to meet Occupational Safety and Health Act requirements.

Georgetown University's cost-per-student for implementing federally mandated social programs rose in seven years from $16 to $356.

Compliance with new regulations on access to buildings for the handicapped could cost higher education as much as $2 billion to modify physical plant. Trinity College in Hartford, Connecticut, is surveying what must be done to its forty-five buildings. It has already seen $75,000 added to the cost of a new dormitory to make it accessible to handicapped. *Trinity has four handicapped students.*

Physical plant modifications needed at the nation's colleges and universities to meet energy efficiency standards and OSHA requirements could cost over *$11 billion.*

But the real threat is to national freedom. The government intrudes into curriculum. Estelle Fishbein, general counsel at Johns Hopkins, emphasizes that, "If regulation of the university inhibits intellectual inquiry, if it suppresses the free exercise of intellectual judgment...then the business of the university is concluded."

We have dwelt on education, but the same tyranny has

clamped onto business, medicine, and volunteer social work. How did this pervasive tyranny invade the land of the free?

The Invasion of
Tuscaloosa County

The invading forces have been easily missed because they have been broken into many small patrols tucked away in dozens of little offices scattered all over the country, deliberately minimizing their presence.

Only recently, as the invaders embolden to build new high-rise office building monuments in which they consolidate their forces, are they becoming really visible.

Since they do not wear uniforms nor hold parades, it is no wonder that we still haven't seen their amazing strength.

But if they were to stage a parade down University Boulevard in Tuscaloosa, you would see 751 Tuscaloosa city employees. They would be followed by 425 Tuscaloosa County employees stationed *only* in Tuscaloosa. They would be followed by 13,000 State of Alabama employees stationed only in Tuscaloosa County. They would be followed by 1,585 *federal* employees stationed *only* in Tuscaloosa County.

Federal? Yes.

We do not include in this parade the municipal employees of the twenty other municipalities in Tuscaloosa County, as we are running out of street. Nor do we include tax-supported public school staffs.

If this were a statewide parade, consider the length of it.

There would be 198,700 state and local government employees. There would be 59,223...repeat,59,223...federal employees stationed in Alabama, not including military.

Thus an army of occupation of 257,923 governs an Alabama citizenry of only 3,665,000 at this writing, a ratio of about 1:14.

Tuscaloosa County is not an extreme example.

In the four-county industrialized area of Ohio (Cuyahoga, Geauga, Lake, Medina), the largest single employer is the federal government—21,000 people.

Just up the Cuyahoga River is Summit County. If occasion would persuade the occupying forces there to parade, we would see 3,305 Akron city employees, followed by 16,767 employees of Summit County and the other towns in the county. They would be followed by the 2,084 State of Ohio people and 2,012 feds stationed in Summit County.

If it were a statewide review, it would include 640,037 people, not counting the military or educators. That is a lot of force to govern only 11 million Ohioans.

Across the nation, not counting armed forces, this army of occupation makes up about 20 percent of our work force.

The secret battalions. Just when we think we have good intelligence reports on the strength of the occupation army, we find we don't. We think we have the federal force accurately logged at about 2.8 million. Suddenly we find there is an invisible, uncountable force that does not show on federal payrolls but is paid very directly by the federal government.

This hidden army works on the payroll of companies that do a lot of work for the government, with federal funds specifically earmarked to pay their salaries. *The National Journal,* published privately in Washington, arrives at an estimate of about 8 million such workers.

Living off the land. Leaving aside the crippling costs (see Chapter 4), the larger threat is that this army of occupation has now become so huge that, no matter how well intended, it must now *first* think of its *own* support systems... an all-consuming project. Hence government *of* the government, *by* the government, *for* the government.

To live off the land, this largest monolithic segment of the population must first look to its own health. That is another reason it is hard for you to detect the massiveness of the occupying force. Apparently it is a rather sickly army. So much so that they have what are called paid sick days, and they generally use every one of them.

Government salaries have risen faster than industry's and lead inflation.

Former Treasury Secretary William W. Simon states that government today accounts for 35¢ of every dollar spent, and that at present rates of increase, it will reach 60¢ by 1985.

So government for the government is now emphatically the major project of this nation.

Government for the government. In taking care of themselves, this army of occupation is so efficient that Senator William Proxmire has tried to cut them back a little by introducing the Limousine Limitations Act. He discovered that 175 government officials were being driven to and from work and other places in limousines at taxpayer cost of $5 million. That includes individual driver salaries of $30,000 per year. Former HEW Secretary Califano's driver received over $38,000 per year.

Journalist M. Stanton Evans came out with Evans' Law of Politics: *"After our people get to the point when they can do us some good, they stop being our people."* They are looking out for themselves.

Our government people travel well. Scripps Howard writers report, for example, that Senator Vance Hartke (Ind.) spent $565 of your money for hotel rooms and meals on a ten-day trip to London. That's not too bad. But he drew $750 from another appropriation that covers overseas travel of congressmen. In addition, he drew $1,883 from a third fund earmarked for congressional travel to cover ground transport. This is over and above the air travel costs from other monies we furnished him. That is good style.

In addition to traveling well, the occupying army is properly trained in protecting itself against the native population with heavy security arrangements. The public is scrutinized upon entering the occupiers' formidable buildings. In the SEC office in the new thirty-eight story Federal Building in Cleveland, "The door is kept locked at all times," according to Oragio Sipari, the attorney-in-charge. "Security is prevalent here and across the country.

"The main job of the SEC is to police [note the word]securities dealers in Ohio."

On the salary side, the occupation army compensates itself well. The CIA hired a retired Navy captain as public relations director at $47,500. He, Herbert E. Hetu, already receives $13,750 a year pension for his twenty-four years' Navy service. So he draws $61,254 which, when he started, was only $5,000 less than a full cabinet officer's.

There are about 141,800 military retirees reemployed by the federal government.

The army of occupation pays its troops generally better than comparable civilian professionals, according to a study from Princeton University headed by Sharon P. Smith. For example, Rex Granum, an Atlanta newpaperman, tripled his salary when he went to work for the White House as deputy press secretary.

Additionally, cost-of-living raises plus 1½ percent are built in. And overgrading, according to Fred Holweg, salary specialist for Civil Service, costs us a least $500 million a year.

Besides the cost burden on the citizen, what is the objection to super-pay for government people? They lose touch with Americans. They have made Washington, D.C., our most affluent city. Bryce Nelson, *New York Times* writer, interviewed a White House aide, a Mr. Follows, who was quitting to take a lower paid job in private industry. The young aide explained, "Isn't there danger to the republic in a mandarin governing class significantly more privileged than the people they are governing?"

The Washington area was number one in median family income among the top twenty cities, 42 percent above prosperous Los Angeles.

Families with combined incomes of $40,000-$60,000 are common in the capital.

Realtors say it is difficult to find a three-bedroom house for $125,000.

The mandarin society extends far beyond Washington to the command posts in other cities where the feds have their deluxe perquisites, including reserved free parking or discounted parking and heavily discounted lunches.

From this artificial elite environment of high-security, high-pay, and low-cost privileges, it is nearly impossible for a government employee to understand the problems of the citizens they regulate.

Congress is growing its own bureaucracy. Senator William Proxmire's monthly Golden Fleece award for stupid spending has been awarded to Congress itself for a 270 percent "eruption of its staff payroll in ten years." Federal legislators now employ

18,400 aides, "Additional staff generates additional bills and work. The added staff is then used to justify new buildings, more restaurants, more parking spaces."

Senator Barry Goldwater complains, "Staff runs Congress. You get off the elevator to vote, and you have to beat your way through fifty or sixty of them standing around."

Former Ohio Senator Frank Lausche operated with eighteen staffers. Senator John Glenn has seventy-one.

The permanent army of occupation has established procedures to make sure there is little chance for the natives' *elected* officials to get rid of them. Nearly every new president opens a campaign to thin out the bureaucracy...and soon finds they can't be fired.

Before a manager can discharge a nonperforming federal worker, he must furnish a written explanation thirty days in advance. The employee may appeal that notice up the chain of command. If the decision is sustained, he may then demand a hearing before a Federal Employee Appeals authority. If that goes against him, he can then appeal to the federal courts.

It has been estimated that to fire a single employee may require 25 percent to 50 percent of a manager's time for six to eighteen months, at a cost to the taxpayers of $100,000. By that time, the manager's own efficiency rating will be suffering. Therefore the experienced manager makes no attempt to fire an employee but gets him transferred to a *turkey farm* department.

Karen House of the *Wall Street Journal* told of an economist the new administration wanted to fire in its drive to clean out dead wood. The $25,000-a-year HUD economist admitted point blank he was actually doing no work on the job except writing freelance articles. When dressed down by his new boss, the economist warned that the civil service regulations made it impossible to fire him. The new HUD supervisor, "I'll spend whatever time it takes."

The economist dared him to try. "I'll wait you out like I did all the others."

It is easier to send the incompetent employee to a turkey farm and hire a new one to replace him. And so the army of occupation grows.

The Elite

The statement that the government's first priority is to take care of itself might be dismissed as diatribe...until we look at the facts. "Survival is the strongest urge in government," said former Agriculture Secretary Earl Butz.

That department is a good example. It was established just over one hundred years ago with nine employees with a specific mission: "To procure, propagate and distribute among the people new and valuable seeds and plants."

Today the number of farmers is rapidly declining, but the Department of Agriculture continues growing. It now has 80,000 full-time employees, one to every thirty-four farmers, plus 45,000 part-timers. It occupies five huge buildings in Washington, D.C., and 16,000 across the nation.

It grows by inventing new programs *while preserving dead programs.*

Item: Its employees measure planted acreage for dozens of crops despite the fact that acreage limitations on plantings have been discontinued.

Item: The Rural Electrification Administration was born in the Depression to get rural America electrified. Today, 99 percent of farms have electricity, but REA is still growing.

Dozens of such programs are perpetuated, while the new programs are sickening even to the employees. Paul Beattie spent much of a year writing standards for watermelons, which he considered make-work because "most consumers know a good watermelon when they see one." And few are going to read a book before buying a melon.

Research projects of negative value abound. One $45,000 study explored how much time Americans spend cooking breakfast. In the works are studies for lunch and dinner.

But the crime is the number of programs devoted simply to justifying expansion of the department. For example, a couple of years back, Mr. Dalton Wilson was drawing a $28,000 salary. One year's project for Mr. Dalton was a study assessing the adequacy and timeliness of the department's literature on fats and oils.

Government public relations. Like any invader, the elite keep themselves elite by making us pay for blatant public relations to tell us how useful the invaders are to us.

The Department of Agriculture employs 600 publicists to write and publish 3500 press releases and 70 TV films telling us of their good works. That cost us $16 million. Another $16 million goes to printing 45 million books, brochures, and pamphlets for the general public. As Senator Ribicoff once said, "The federal government suffers from runaway flacksterism."

An estimated 19,000 federal government flacks under the thin euphemism "government communicators" assail all media with stories of government's good works at a payroll cost of about $400 million per year.

A Library of Congress study discovered that in six months federal agencies published 102,000 different promotional brochures to impress us. The annual printing bill for this avalanche of PR material is $1.5 billion.

The dialogue in these in-house PR departments is the same type of chatter you hear in regular commercial PR agencies, with one blatant difference. The speakers seem totally unaware that they are actually using the client's own money to sell the client on themselves.

The efficiency with which the occupying army of elite looks out for itself at the expense of the natives is awesome.

In inflationary times when citizens struggle to pay rising prices amid rising unemployment, the elite acquire for themselves more deluxe freebies.

Item: 15,000 federal employees get free or low-cost parking privileges ($6.60 per month) near their offices. Cost to taxpayers: $11 million yearly.

Item: 500 Defense Department top management people eat subsidized lunches in five white linen executive dining rooms with appetizer, dessert, and beverage for about $2.00.

Item: Congressmen and their staffs buy at huge discount from the House Stationery Store a wide variety of household items including children's books, luggage, jewelry. Many also get free haircuts and house plants and free tax preparation service at taxpayer expense.

Item: Former Attorney General Saxbe had a private dining room and a manservant near his office and traveled with four bodyguards.

Item: The government maintains two resorts in national parks for federal brass, one in Shenandoah National Park and a mansion in Grand Teton Park, Wyoming.

High cost is not the chief evil of creating a mandarin elite. The disaster relates to freedom. The occupying elite become arrogant toward the natives.

Norman Mlachak of the *Cleveland Press* entered the Federal Courthouse, which he had helped pay for, in Cleveland to cover a story.

"I was confronted by one of four armed guards. He made me empty my pockets—keys, coins, wallet, lighter—[and]strip off my jacket." After the X-raying, Mlachak was frisked. It wasn't the act that rankled so much as the attitude of the elite.

"It's typical of the demeaning and *contemptuous* reception citizens get from the United States of America.... It's a grim and frightening reflection of what the government thinks of its citizens.

"Instead of being confronted with an atmosphere that bespeaks the grandeur and majesty of the laws...we're greeted with suspicion, fear, distrust, and hostility.

"All doors but one are locked—even one for the handicapped.

"Another ukase besmirching the marble pillar outside the chambers of Judge Battisti even specifies what citizens must wear in his court: coat, shirt, tie, trousers, socks, shoes.

"That's what the Nixon gang wore. It was not the uniform of the day for tens of thousands of young men the nation sent to their deaths in Viet Nam.

"The courthouse atmosphere is sick and despairing and frightening. A nation where the government looks with distrust and suspicion of its citizens, and with contempt.

"That's how low we have fallen."

The elitism goes way beyond contempt for our dignity to contempt for our liberty and our lives.

Operation Seaspray. Norman Cousins, editor of the *Saturday Review,* documents in the November 10, 1979, issue an event in which the Army carried out 239 open air bacteriological tests in San Francisco, New York, Key West, and Panama City, Florida.

In one of these tests, the Navy, in cooperation with the Army, sprayed the San Francisco Bay area for six days with serratia, a bacteria that causes a pneumonia. One of the three objectives was "to study the offensive possibilities of attacking a seaport city with BW [biological warfare]."

Fortunately for us, the program was only as effective as most government work. Even so, twelve people were treated for serratia pneumonia at one hospital, Stanford University. Edward Nevins, a pipefitter, died. His descendants are now suing for $11 million.

The outrage is not how many people were sickened, but a government so elite that, without even informing the citizens, it presumes to experiment with their lives.

From congressional hearings, we now know that AEC officials in charge of nuclear tests in Nevada never warned the people in downwind St. George about the probability of heavy fallout from those tests.

Following leukemia cases in St. George, Governor Scott Mattheson of Utah described the cover-up by AEC officials as "an incredibly irresponsible course of conduct."

But if you say, you can still pass the violations over, then I ask, Hath your house been burnt? Hath your property been destroyed before your face? Are your wife and children destitute of a bed to lie on, or bread to live on? Have you lost a parent or child by their hands, and yourself the ruined and wretched survivor? If you have not, then are you not a judge of those who have. But if you have, and still can shake hands with the murderers, then are you unworthy the name of husband, father, friend, or lover, and whatever may be your rank or title in life, you have the heart of a coward, and the spirit of a sycophant.

—Common Sense

"An Alien Government"

My government doesn't seem to like me. Baylor University President Abner McCall is a big shambling friendly American who loves Texas and loves America with a great Airedale affection and a huge following of friends. He was asked to address a group of congressmen and highly placed government people in Washington. The message he had for them was a shocker, delivered in quiet, sad tones. The U.S. government is illegitimate.

Citing former United Nations Ambassador Andrew Young's pronouncement that the government of South Africa was illegitimate, he said, "I presume that Mr. Young meant that it did not represent the majority of the people, that they did not accept it as their government, and that they felt little or no loyalty to it. You know, to me that seems a pretty good description of the federal government of the United States.

"There are millions of us out there who no longer feel the federal government is really our government. We do not believe it represents our best interests. We do not believe it responds to our wishes. We remember the observation of sociologist Robert Michels on the iron law of oligarchy, that power issuing from the people ends by raising itself above the people.

"Many of us now feel the federal has so far departed from its original source of power, the people, that it might well be ...classified illegitimate. It has so twisted and flagrantly violated its original grant of power, the Constitution, that it has forfeited its claim to legitimacy.

"*To many of us it is an alien government*. . . . We love our country, but we do not identify our government with our country. . . .

"Watergate, the sex scandals, Koreagate, were...nothing beside the arrogance and oppression from thousands of bureaucrats. . . . My government doesn't seem to like me."

Government by the government. But none of this quite reveals the final raw power of the governmental army of occupation. Through it all the natives have felt that at least the private citizen still initiated the legislation via elected representatives.

Few have noticed that the initiative has shifted. The public sector now initiates the legislation which as bureaucrats it will then administer.

One of the first to sound this alarm has been Professor Samuel Beer of Harvard. He explains *how most new legislation now emerges from the bureaucracy itself.*

How could that be possible?

Each federal bureau wishing to initiate a piece of legislation and pressure the Congress to pass it has developed a huge voter constituency. For example, the federal military organizations have a vast shadow constituency in the civilian military production industries. The government health bureaus project to a large private health industry. The government education bureaucrats can amass broad support from public school personnel. The post office has an army of voters on its own payroll reaching into every town. The welfare bureaucrats appeal to an enormous constituency to support their legislative initiatives. It is a bold congressman who would vote against such blocs.

The army of occupation has made a complete coup to the point where it not only administers the laws, *it makes the laws.*

When the people perceive this, they turn to candidates who run on anti-Washington programs. But when these talented and bright newcomers come to the government town, they find themselves helpless. The nonelected professionals are fully in charge. Benevolently they allow the newcomers to take a few legislative initiatives, but nothing really affecting the bureaus.

So we see an elite army of occupation looking out for its own pay, its own comforts, its own security, its own baggage train, and its own perpetuation by legislation.

But there is more—and worse. An elite force must have some work mission for the legions. This work must have the ring of high purpose to sustain the self-esteem and arrogance of the occupying troops, just as their pillage of the land sustains their bellies.

This high purpose must always at least *begin* with the intention of helping the people. That is where the real trouble starts.

What big government strives to help, it hurts. What it tries to save, it kills.

. . . that the same tyranny which drove the first emigrants from home, pursues their descendents still.

—Common Sense

The Government as Enemy
The Carrot vs. the Big Stick

"Never blame a legislative body for not doing something," Will Rogers said. "When they do nothing, they don't hurt anybody. When they do something is when they become dangerous."

Our government has become dangerous. It now tries to do *everything*. This is an exact reversal of our strongest days.

The heart of the matter is the carrot vs. the big stick.

In the early days of the weak republic, our fragile government coordinated a war of rebellion against England, then possessor of the largest and most dangerous naval fleet in history. The republic had not enough money in the treasury at one time to pay a $1500 bill for cannon, let alone build a single warship.

What should our government do?

It made the shrewdest naval maneuver in history. It offered a carrot to the private shipping business. The government wrote out on very fancy paper a commission for any qualified private vessel to serve as privateer in the service of the infant republic. Armed with this certificate, the privateer vessel was authorized to attack and capture any British ship in defined "American waters." The privateer was authorized to keep any booty recovered from a British ship.

What did that do? From a standing start, that carrot created an instant navy of such powerful motivation that it swept British shipping from our shores. The charter was so generously phrased concerning "American waters" that this aggressive young civilian navy not only chased out British shipping, but pursued it halfway home in fast vessels used in American trade.

Our government thus learned early that when it comes to getting a huge project accomplished, give private citizens an incentive and the job will be accomplished. Enlist the ingenuity, imagination, creativity, and ambition of the citizens, and the government's work is *done*.

The young republic next needed settlers to hold the West, which England, Spain, and then Mexico still expected to retrieve. (England did not abandon its western forts at the close of the Revolution.)

Again, the weak American government turned to citizens with a carrot. It sold at friendly prices vast tracts of land to town builders like Jonathan Dayton, John Young, and Isaac Zane on condition that they people it with settlers who could hold the land until the fragile republic could raise another army. This carrot created in the then West hundreds of towns like Dayton and Youngstown and Zanesville, Ohio.

Next we needed roads.

Again the carrot. The government authorized citizens to build private turnpikes and collect tolls from the traffic. Suddenly roads appeared.

Still later, settlers were needed farther west. The government used the carrot. It offered public lands to individual citizens on condition they settle the land, build a cabin, and get a crop in. A land rush followed.

Another carrot. The government offered alternate sections of land to railroad companies along the right-of-way if they would build railroads. And soon we had a rail network extending across the continent.

Thus the government offered its citizens incentive, and *their* drive, ingenuity, and ambition accomplished huge works.

As Vermont Royster put it in the *Wall Street Journal* (January 31, 1979), "Historically our economic growth was built on imaginative innovation not only in products but in production methods. By the end of World War II, our major industries— autos, for example, or steel—were preeminent; the world begged for their products."

Today, by self-inflicted wounds from our own government, we are losing out in the automotive fields, and our steel industry is in jeopardy.

The National Science Foundation reports that foreign inventions now account for nearly one-third of the 1300 patents issued each week by the U.S. Patent Office.

The catalog of industries lost from the United States to foreign nations is staggering.

Vanishing innovation in the United States is a major cause for alarm in all fields of endeavor.

While foreign governments are offering incentives to their people, the United States government has abandoned the carrot and adopted the big stick.

Sam W. Tinsley is director of corporate technology for Union Carbide Corporation. He remarks, "Government officials keep asking us 'Where are the golden eggs?' while the other part of their apparatus is beating hell out of the goose that lays them."

"Vanishing Innovation" in a hostile government climate for new ideas and products was the subject of a series in *Business Week*.

Excessive, coercive, and contradictory government regulatory policy is the single greatest brake on American innovation.

A spokesman for Bell Labs gives an example. "By 1972, a skeletal muscle relaxant marketing permit from the Food and Drug Administration required submitting 456 volumes of test data, each two inches thick—seventy-six feet in total thickness, weighing one ton."

"Regulation," says Tinsley of Union Carbide, "has put a bottleneck on new product development in the industry."

William J. Abernathy of the Harvard Business School states that government policy toward innovation guarantees an obsolescent American industry. The lesson it teaches our citizen businessmen is, "Don't do anything really new; don't change."

The big stick is always wielded in the name of *helping*.

What the government helps, it hurts. A young woman whom Mike Royko, the columnist, calls Sue was looking for work.

Sue was twenty-two, had no job experience; she was divorced and had a two-year-old child. That is not a strong resume for a job. But a lady executive at an employment agency took an interest in Sue, found her intelligent, and managed to land her a job as a beginning clerk.

After six months Sue would get a 10 percent raise. After a year, another 10 percent raise. And the company, Foote, Cone & Belding, a major advertising agency, would send her to night school so she could advance professionally. Sue was pleased and accepted the job. Her married sister would take care of the baby daytimes.

Sue was on her way up and out of the ADC (Aid to Dependent Children) trap.

But on Monday Sue did not arrive on the job. The employment office lady called Sue's home—"Why?" Sue explained that her government welfare caseworker had advised her not to take the job.

Sue said the welfare counselor told her that given her ADC check and the food stamp and the free medical care from welfare, she should consider carefully what was best for her. "By the time I pay my transportation to get downtown and back, I'm not doing any better than I am now with my welfare check and food stamps."

Multiply Sue by tens of thousands of Americans getting that kind of help into dependency.

The federal government set out to help Miss Bessie Heppner, age sixty-eight; but now they are hurting her.

Dolores Orman reported the story in the Ft. Myers, Florida, *News-Press* under the headlines: "Catch 22. Miss Heppner Loses Benefits by Saving Too Much Money."

A hipbone ailment forced Miss Heppner to quit work in 1972. She had saved $700 from her work as a domestic laundry worker. She went on Social Security ($94 per month). Because of her hip injury and the smallness of her savings, she was approved for an additional $130 per month from SSI (Supplemental Security Income program for the aged, blind, and disabled with little or no income).

Miss Heppner lived very frugally and put some of this in the bank in case she might face some unexpected emergency. The government later asked for her bankbook, and then notified her that her savings exceeded the allowable limit of $1,500. Her SSI payments were being discontinued.

Miss Heppner said, "I didn't know I wasn't allowed to save the money."

She had made most of her purchases at sales, using coupons from the Thursday newspaper, the only paper she buys. By Spartan frugality she had saved $2,300 against future emergency. An attorney, Peter Braun, became incensed about her treatment. "Because she elected to show wisdom and save money she's being punished." Braun argued before Judge Avram Weisberger that the $1,500 ceiling on savings "was intended by Congress to mean savings *other than* SS or SSI money.

"By restricting her savings they are putting a limit on how she spends her grant," which they can't legally do.

Weisberger agreed and so ruled. However, the Appeals Council of Social Security Administration reversed Weisberger.

Meanwhile Miss Heppner survives on her $94 Social Security check.

Multiply Miss Heppner by millions, and what kind of country do we have?

The government set out to help James Howard Kunstler. Kunstler is author of *I Was a CETA Goldbrick.* CETA stands for Comprehensive Employment Training Act. The act's purpose is to reduce unemployment, furnishing temporary jobs to unemployed people like Kunstler, while training them for permanent jobs elsewhere.

Kunstler got himself hired onto a CETA staff of five people involved in parks recreation. He was called a recreation assistant at $120 per week; and he was ready, willing, and expecting to plunge into an intensive program with all his energy.

What was the department's work? Kunstler was told the mission was "to come up with new ideas to make the public parks more accessible to the disadvantaged, handicapped, elderly, and general public."

Kunstler read a report showing what progress had been made in the previous six months. One item was the "senior citizens' kazoo concert." Fourteen people came. One was a "New Games Festival." Twenty-two people came. There were four other programs of this caliber put on by a staff drawing $46,500 in salaries during the six months.

From the day Kunstler arrived on the job, no one asked him to do any work. So after thirty days Kunstler brought his portable typewriter into the office and began to write a book. No one disturbed him. He found others working on private projects.

After two months, the group was moved into new carpeted quarters with a private office for each staffer. This made it easier for each to pursue a personal project. Kunstler finished a novel and resigned. "In more than three months on the job, I had hardly done any work except for personal gain." He'd received no training for any permanent job. He had learned cynicism toward government assistance, in his words "a fraud."

Multiply Kunstler by hundreds of thousands "helped" in destructive government programs.

Lynn Thompson had a severe crippling affliction that entitled her to Social Security funds to hire an aide to assist her with her wheelchair and certain mechanical gear for sustaining life. Lynn was classified "totally dependent."

That classification bothered her.

A very bright girl, she studied accounting by correspondence. Finally she acquired a few very small clients who would bring their monthly financial paperwork to her house so she could do their books. There were not enough clients yet to support her, but a future was building.

However, the Social Security Administration discovered that

she was no longer *"totally* dependent." They wrote her that she would have to pay back all monies previously provided and could receive no more.

Lynn Thompson left a note: *"I've got everything in order. Got a letter from Social Security about overpayment. Not sleeping well at night. I love you all very much."*

What the government helps, it often kills.

The assassination of citizen initiative. Seventy-six-year-old Margaret Toy became aware of a large population among us unable to prepare a decent meal at home and deprived of any society at mealtime. Alone, they munched candy bars and cold cereal. They were perishing from lack of nutrition and especially mealtime companionship.

Margaret Toy imported a great idea from England—Meals on Wheels. Today in large communities all over the United States sociable volunteers deliver meals on wheels to lonesome homes and, more important, a side dish of human companionship. The meals are not free, except in cases of poverty.

Today Margaret Toy is dismayed. The government thinks it could do this job better. Under the Older Americans Act, the government is moving in. They have a lot of improvements to offer on delivering meals to the aged.

There is a $50 billion dollar operation in this country manned by what John D. Rockefeller III called "the Third Sector," namely volunteers. Thirty-seven million of us are involved. The nation deep down believes that neighbors, not governments, should take care of neighbors. Volunteerism is more efficient, more compassionate, more perceptive—and not coercive.

Volunteer philanthropy uncovers the needs. For example, wealthy society doctor James Turpin became aware that any young doctor could handle advising his affluent California patients to lose thirty pounds, whereas advanced medical skill was needed by moneyless men and women dying in Tennessee because they *really* needed an excellent doctor.

Turpin sold two boats and other adult toys and outfitted a van as a clinic. He created Project Concern. Putting the arm on other wealthy doctors to volunteer their services for four-week hitches, he drives medicine into the Tennessee mountains. He charges each patient $1.00, whether for heart trouble or acne.

Today Project Concern is an international operation supported by thousands of small philanthropists.

In nearly every town somebody starts a volunteer operation to take care of the blind, the crippled, the retarded...to build a hospital, a home for the aged, a church, a gym, a symphony hall.

Thirty-seven million of us are volunteering time and/or money to uncounted volunteer organizations to find runaway kids, help alcoholics, man drug control centers, teach the kids woodsmanship, help the crippled, lonely, and abandoned, shelter the aged, research catastrophic disease. We supply everything from money to labor to whole blood.

The list is interminable. And in a very real sense, *this* is the best thing Americans do.

Lest we underestimate the weight of volunteer operations, take just one example—the work of the Women's Association of Morristown Memorial Hospital in New Jersey. They provided in one year 885 volunteers who put in 145,000 hours on forty-five services to the hospital, and raised over $1 million for hospital equipment.

"Throughout our history," Rockefeller further points out, "virtually every significant step in social progress sprang from the third sector [volunteerism]."

The list is long, and it includes Margaret Toy's Meals on Wheels.

Now...the government wants in. What do untrained lay people know?

If we shut down volunteerism in this country, government will charge in to fill the void at a tremendous cost in dollars, and at a bigger cost in the loss of the national volunteer attitude.

Volunteers and volunteer organizations have been able to carry on their massive works because of the tax exemption carrot allowed for philanthropic contribution. That huge incentive may be destroyed by movements in Congress to modify and even eliminate charitable tax credit incentive. The government now turns to the stick.

Yet the greatest lift America could experience would be a major increase in volunteerism. What the government helps, it hurts.

Item: The government wanted to help the employees of small companies get pension plans of a certain standard. It therefore came out with a 247-page regulation on how small companies shall conduct their employee pension plans. It made pension administration so costly, complex, and confusing that 13,000 small companies immediately canceled their pension plans. The victim? The people government tried to help.

Item: The well-intended minimum wage increase in one year reduced teenage employment by 320,000. The victim: young people the government tried to help.

Item: Everyone is in favor of clean air. No argument. But after 94 percent of emissions have been removed, the government wants another 3 percent removed even though the cost equals that of the first 94 percent. Clean air becomes very brutal economics. Direct result: 351 foundries gave their employees final notice. Couldn't cut it. Shut down. Those employees walked across the street to collect unemployment compensation. The casualty? The people.

Item: The federal government alone now operates 1,200 regulatory boards, commissions, and committees, most of which have enforcement powers. They are subduing Americans with the big stick and charging us for their ineffectiveness with enormous taxes. (See Chapter 4.)

How to Lick the Invading Army

Number One: Refuse government help.

Whenever the government comes up with a new plan that says, "We want to help you," organize vigorous refusal.

Big government needs both a big vote and big money to exist. When voting, we need to consider whether the candidate's attitude and actions favor the efficient carrot or the costly stick.

Society in every state is a blessing, but government even in its best state is but a necessary evil: in its worst state an intolerable one. . . and he will take from your fields and your olive yards, even the best of them, and give them to his servants. . . .

—Common Sense

The famous Alexis de Tocqueville wrote a friendly account of the United States during the 1830s, but he concluded, "This young republic will probably endure until its politicians learn that its people can be bribed with their own money."

That is exactly where we are now.

Hence we must resist government assistance. It is very hard to do.

The federal revenue-sharing machinery forced $1,198 on Lazy Lakes, Florida. Lazy Lakes did not ask for the money and does not want it. It has taken them two years to shut off the checks from the government.

Government's role should be harshly confined to basic security.

Two: Fight back.

Remember Joe Pinga of West Warwick, Rhode Island? He could pay the $90 fine imposed on his bakery by OSHA better than he could afford the legal costs of opposing it. But he thought it important to fight back. He paid $1,500 in legal fees to take the United States government to court.

The young woman OSHA inspector wept on the witness stand, admitting her only qualification for charging Joe Pinga was forty hours of OSHA seminars. Despite her tears, Joe felt she represented raw danger. He pounded a thick OSHA regulation book—"That's not America."

He should know. His father came here at great cost when America represented freedom.

Charles MacKenzie, president of Grove City College in Grove City, Pennsylvania, ignored HEW's Form 639A (Assurance of compliance with the sexual discrimination provision of Title IX). This form applies to colleges receiving federal funds. MacKenzie knew Grove City had no sex discrimination, but he also wanted no federal aid. So HEW Form 639A did not apply.

But HEW said it did. Individual students were receiving over $700,000 a year in government student loans and grants. Unless MacKenzie filled out 639A, HEW would cut off these funds.

MacKenzie and four students sued to block HEW.

Judge Paul Simmons of the Pittsburgh Federal District Court ruled in favor of Grove City and decreed that the government had no legal right to penalize individual students "as a remedy for coercing a college."

Ferrol G. (Bill) Barlow is a small plumbing contractor in Po-

catello, Idaho. His face is lined by hard work, and his office wall is decorated with a framed copy of the Bill of Rights.

On a very busy day an inspector from OSHA (Occupational Safety and Health Administration) showed up unannounced to inspect Barlow's shop. Barlow told him no.

A series of court actions led to the Supreme Court. In June of 1978, that court ruled 5–3 that employers can bar government inspectors who do not have a warrant.

Three: Support every version of a sunset law.

Many towns, states, and the federal government are striving to put limits on new agencies and bureaus and government organizations at the time of their creation so that the organization automatically goes out of business at a prescribed point in time. To extend its life, it must justify it all over again.

Wherever you find a legislator at any level trying to build the sunset into any law, jump to his support.

Four: Support every effort to supplant government services with private suppliers. It is happening. Give it a boost.

North Olmsted, Ohio, disbanded its rubbish operation and gave it to a private contractor, Brotherton Refuse. Joseph Corrigan, North Olmsted service director, reports, "I don't know what it is, but they are doing the same work in the same way a lot cheaper than we could ever hope to do it." The city department costs were $971,000 per year. The private contractor charges $468,000. The North Olmsted city department required seven three-man crews to handle the rubbish collection; the Brotherton Company does the job with three two-man crews.

Does reducing rubbishmen have anything to do with our freedom? Emphatically. It diminishes the troops of the new invading army.

Five: Support every movement to overhaul civil service. Several are under way. Watch for others. Wisconsin has approved a sweeping overhaul of its state civil service. Oregon's legislature voted to remove three hundred top positions from civil service. New York and Kansas are in the middle of comprehensive review of their civil service to make career service more responsive to elected officials.

The universal problem with present systems is that exemplary service goes unrewarded while mediocre performance is protected with a lifetime tenure.

It's an old joke, but don't stop us if you've heard it:

Why is a civil service worker like a wet firecracker?

It won't work, and you can't fire it.

Of course, it isn't really that funny, is it?

2

MORE TAKE-HOME PAY

THE BEST KEPT SECRETS

ABOUT WORKING

"Why is it better for a youngster to be unemployed at $3.20
per hour than to be employed at $2.00?"
—*Walter Williams*

This is a chapter of surprises, with one wallbanger at the end. But don't skip to the last page. Hang onto your prejudices until you get there... if you can.

In the woods in Intervale, New Hampshire, seventy miles from the nearest place you ever heard of, is a red barn. No advertising helps people find it. A small sign obscured by foliage says, "Limmer & Sons, Custom Shoemakers."

Inside the barn is the family of Peter Limmer, who came here from Bavaria. There's Frank Limmer, his brother Peter, his son Karl, his nephew Stephen, and his wife, Maria. They're making boots for foresters, farmers, mountaineers, and backpackers.

You have to send a tracing of your feet, and then you're supposed to go for a try-on later.

But you can't place an order at this writing. Every time their backlog climbs up to three years work, the Limmers cut off orders.

At a time when the American shoe industry has been driven out of business by foreign shoemakers, the Limmers have just cut off new orders again. These orders come from all over the world to the Limmers' barn. They have a secret magic—they make good boots.

The wonderful surly arrogance of a workman who knows he does good work is real freedom.

Work has been our best friend.

Men and women from all over the world have gone through hell in leaking boats—and still do—to get to this country for the freedom to work and the freedom to choose their own line of work.

Until fairly recently we ran the nation in such a way that the unfettered inventive ideas and energies and ambition of millions of working people were free to build the greatest free society in history.

Today—no.

We are destroying our greatest strength—the workplace—with self-inflicted wounds.

Samuel Gompers would be shocked. Gompers, one of labor history's handful, created the American Federation of Labor. Way ahead of his time, the great labor leader's tremendous authority over three-acre crowds assembled in open fields came because his courage and his intellectual reach projected quickly. In a voice that could almost peel tree bark, the distinguished labor leader pushed his message to the edge of the fields and beyond; "The objective of labor is. . .MORE!"

And that is still the objective. . .and properly so.

The challenge today, however, is *how to get more.*

Gompers would be startled to see that we are still using his same strategies, although the work world and the economy and the society have totally changed.

Gompers would have changed techniques.

Although we brag that our modern labor leader is an MBA with possibly a side degree in law, and that the modern corporate industrial relations manager is sophisticated in labor history, we are still carrying on an archaic civil war among the two sets of people best qualified to collaborate on the direct route to *more.*

Gompers would surely see that the raise the working man needs now is not more inflated paper dollars, but more buying power.

It's common sense.

Not to be so hard on our MBA union leader and our corporate manager—they both know that, too. And they know how to get it. More productivity.

Then what stops them?

Credibility.

Gus Kish Does Not Believe

The union leader's reelection and the corporate manager's career depend upon people like Gus Kish. *And he does not believe.* That is our big problem.

"I don't believe it. I don't believe it *yet*." Hearth maintenance man, Gus Kish, age sixty, was talking to colleagues in the Open Hearth Bar on Steel Street, Youngstown, Ohio.[1] He had just learned that next week he would be unemployed. "We've all been hearing the plant was gonna close for the last thirty years, but I never thought I'd see the day...."

Kish didn't believe it.

Yet whenever a union secures for its members wages that price the product out of the market, the result is a pretty contract to reprint in the union newspaper...and unemployment. Gus Kish has the newspaper...and he is unemployed.

Union leadership understands why. But Kish is their constituency, and he does not believe the signals.

There is a clear route to get *more* for Gus Kish, but he probably will not reelect the union official who takes that clear route.

We Americans have put on blinders to shut out a glaring truth. Under the spell of government and union voices, we and Gus Kish convinced ourselves that somehow we could keep on paying ourselves more than we're earning—10 percent raises with a 1.5 percent increase in the productivity. Judging from his remarks in the Open Hearth Bar, Kish sincerely seems to believe that.

Then what's wrong with management that they can't stand up to unworkable labor costs?

J. Fred Weston, professor in the graduate school of manage-

1. *Cleveland Press,* November 29, 1979.

ment of the University of California at Los Angeles, in testimony before the International Trade Commission, showed that in the 1950s and 1960s, the federal government intervened so heavily in steel industry-labor negotiations always finding in favor of the union, that steel industry management finally gave up. They "broke the back of industry resistance to high wage demands." Hence the steel business went overseas.

Steel is used here only as an example. You could as easily speak of autos, motorcycles, clothes, shoes, electronic appliances, or sporting goods.

Samuel Gompers said, "The object of labor...is *more!*"

To get more, would he stand by and watch industry leave America? Is that common sense?

But Gus Kish's idea, as expressed in the Open Hearth Bar in Youngstown, is...make the government "shut out that foreign stuff."

A man with a mermaid flexing on a twenty-inch forearm replied, "That just means U.S. prices will all go up as high as they want."

"Then *control* the prices."

But free trade *is* the best price control. Our ability to meet free trade price competition and still turn a profit is the way to know we are measuring up in productivity effectiveness.

Free trade forces the *more* that Gompers wanted for the working man. And it is at the same time the perfect price control.

Gompers, a self-taught economist, taught his union members to make the natural laws of economics work for them just as farmers use the laws of nature.

It is time for a modern Gompers.

An Unmentionable Subject

The facts of life about wage raises are that they can *viably* come from only one source, increased productivity.

Wage raises by any other means create inflation, which offsets the raise. Wage raises by government edict create both inflation and unemployment.

Increased productivity does *not* generally mean men working harder or faster. It generally means increased output resulting from increased capital invested in tools per workman. Put a ten horsepower motor at the end of a man's arm, and he can turn out more work than when he had a quarter-horse-power motor.

Give a plastics pressman a ten-opening press, he can turn out more sheets of plastic laminate than a man with a five-opening plastics press. The difference is not how hard the man works, but how much money you can put into his tools.

In the middle 1970s, capital investment per worker in the United States grew only 0.6 percent per year, compared to 2.19 percent over the previous twenty-two years.

The contrast with our competition is scary. As of this writing, German productivity is growing 4 percent per year; Japanese at 7 percent per year. The Japanese reinvest nearly 20 percent of their GNP in plant and equipment with a labor force that is not growing.

Around the world, the greatest social progress has always come from stepping up the capital investment per worker—new tooling and plant expansion.

"Then why tell me about it?" Gus Kish would surely ask. "What does the working man have to do with the formation of capital?"

Almost everything.

Of the several sources of capital formation for a company, the soundest source is profit. In the case of Kish's company and other steel companies, profit is a decreasing resource. They are no longer favored bank loan customers, nor is their stock attractive to investors.

Insofar as the working man restricts his company from making profit, he inhibits capital formation. The workman can work hard and, with coercive work rules, work stretch-out provisions, and crippling raises, still throttle his company's ability to make a profit. Additionally, by sponsoring and supporting antibusiness legislation, with his tremendous political clout, he can derail his company from profitability.

Gompers would consider this suicidal.

That brings us to a second high voltage word—*unionism.* Practically everyone understands the necessity and importance of unions. But union techniques for trying to better the worker's life still come down to decreasing output, stretching out the job, and restricting work by rules to offset technological production gains.

The union further restricts productivity by using the enormous clout of the National Labor Relations Board against the productivity of the company paying its union members. Via the NLRB and other government agencies, the union forces upon industry nonproductive machinery for safety and environmental protection way beyond need, thereby reducing productivity.

Yet the viable route to higher pay is clearly higher productivity. The modern union man learned that at business school. The proof that it works is visible. For example, it has been demonstrated by Cleveland's Lincoln Electric Company.

Lincoln Electric Company pays a year-end bonus for productivity at all pay levels and has done so for three decades. These spectacular bonuses are no mere Christmas turkey. They often match or exceed the employee's annual pay. They always make headlines. Recently the company divided $24 million among 2,000 employees.

The company is able to compete with foreign imports on price while paying spectacular wages. The reason in both cases is productivity superiority. More output makes more pay.

C. Jackson Grayson heads the American Productivity Center, Inc., in Houston, Texas. "Productivity is the only tool in our economic arsenal that works positively on both inflation and recession," he explains. "It increases real wages—the amount you have left after you take out the bite of inflation."

Grayson's studies show that the "old technological fear of displacement and being fired simply is not true, except on a temporary basis. Over history, there is a definite correlation between high productivity and high employment."

The Japanese have been coming to the United States to study our productivity for twenty years. "Now they've gone back home," Grayson explains, "and they're beating our brains out with what they learned and we've forgotten."

If we citizens don't correct the productivity output of our nation, our government is going to have to take care of more and more of us unemployed at a lower and lower standard of living; and to do that, government is going to need to adopt stricter powers over us as they divide up among us diminishing food, shelter, and necessities.

What about government productivity? A huge part of the productivity of the citizenry is wiped out by the stupefying unproductivity of government—on all levels—eating up the results of the citizen's labor by massive inefficiency, waste, and lack of performance. This matters because government services are now a huge part of the gross national product. Government spends nearly half the money spent. When government spends, the money goes into consumption items generally, not productive machinery.

In addition, the government has certain work it is supposed to perform for us. It performs this so poorly and unproductively that this also drags down total citizen productivity.

Government is by definition a monopoly, and it is nearly impossible to make a monopoly efficient and productive; it has no competition to spur it.

And then there's the bitter reply that government makes regulations that destroy the productivity of others.

Wherefore, security being the true design and end of government, it unanswerably follows that whatever form thereof appears most likely to ensure it to us, with the least expense and greatest benefit, is preferable to all others.

—Common Sense

Thoughtful men now believe that two moves may help. First, sunset laws, which decommission a government agency at a specific time when its job is done. Second, many feel that what is most needed is a way of measuring the real productivity of an agency. This is not easy. For example, the U.S. Employment Service may be doing exactly what it is commissioned to do at an exemplary rate of speed. We could measure how many unemployed persons the agency interviews, qualifies, trains, and places in jobs. On the other hand, that may not give us a good measure of productivity, because many analysts now suspect that the agency may actually be perpetuating unemployment instead of softening its effects. We need to learn how to measure government productivity.

In measuring the Government Printing Office's productivity, the number of pieces published could be measured easily. But that means nothing. Does the content of the publications do any good?

Probably we have no trouble measuring the productivity of a

government road repair crew. But the majority of our government is involved in enormous unmeasurable abstractions.

Eight Best-Kept Secrets

No. 1: High Productivity Makes High Employment

Two statements are fashionable. One is that higher per man productivity *reduces* employment. The other is that low productivity is in no way the fault of the working man.

In complex macroeconomics, this can get very fuzzy, but on a local level the situation becomes clear.

Thirteen-year-old Bill Acton heard that his friend Sam Naiden was no longer working over at the hardware store, so he rushed right over and asked Mr. T.L. Bedford, "Can I fill Sammy's vacancy?"

Bedford was a gentle man, but matter-of-fact. He said, "Bill, Sammy didn't leave no vacancy."

By contrast, down in Columbus, Ohio, twelve-year-old Eddie Rickenbacker, later president of Eastern Air Lines, applied for work at the Franklin Machine Shop. They told him in the front office there was no work available, and it was unlikely there would be for a boy. Leaving, Eddie took the long route out through the shop to the back door. Looking around, he noticed that the floor was covered with an inch buildup of packed-down machine grease imbedded with metal shavings. As he reached the back door, a steam whistle blew. Lunch time. The men shut down the machines and went outside.

Eddie found a shovel. He chose a production bay about ten feet square and attacked the floor with the shovel, using it as a scraper. He couldn't find a wheelbarrow, but there was a greasy tarp on which he piled the cuttings from the floor and hauled them out back. He carried out nine loads, then fine-tuned his cleaning with a broom. When he was finished, the floor was not spic and span clean, but he was down to the wood...except for a one-foot square he'd left untouched right in the middle.

When the men came back from lunch they looked at the area curiously and at the kid. Somebody must have gone into the front office. The boss came out and looked. He didn't greet Eddie, just walked around looking at the floor and rubbing his chin. Finally he looked up at Eddie and pointed to the untouched square foot in the middle, "Well, why didn't you clean up that island in the middle, too?"

Eddie was a little nervous. "Well, sir, I had to leave it to show you my work made a difference."

The boss went behind the steam boiler and came back with a firebox rake, which he handed to Eddie, "This will work better. You can start tomorrow morning. Seven-thirty."

Work is not kid's stuff. But these two kids demonstrate a best-kept secret of economics. Lack of productivity makes unemployment. Productivity creates jobs.

No. 2: Workers Hurt Workers

From the Ft. Myers *News Press*, April 6, 1979:

TRUCK STRIKE ALARMS CAR MAKERS

DETROIT (AP)—The nation's automakers say the trucking industry labor stalemate threatens to shut down the automobile industry. By Thursday, the automakers said, the combination of strike and industry lockout idled more than 54,000 autoworkers.

"I just hope it doesn't go beyond a week or we'll all be in serious trouble," said President Lee A. Iacocca of Chrysler, which plans to stop all production Monday unless there is a Teamsters' settlement.

The strike threatens to force General Motors to shut its U.S. operations down tight.

Another 89,850 auto workers were working short shifts as car companies struggled with materials shortages.

There have been no layoffs at Ford, but the No. 2 automaker has 51,000 employees at 18 assembly plants working reduced shifts. A company spokesman said it was just a matter of time until shortages trigger layoffs.

The trouble with strikes is that they hurt the wrong people—other workers. They are small editions of civil war. They pit the truck driver against the auto worker, you against me.

Today our economy is so tightly interrelated that an economic injury to one of us quickly spreads out to most of us. A strike like the one headlined above hits the auto worker obviously, but moments later it hits the glassworker in Toledo making windshields, the plastic worker in Connecticut making seat upholstery, the paint worker in Kentucky.

It spreads out fast.

Yet the final damage is not quite so obvious to Gus Kish. During the lull in production of domestic autos and steel, the Japanese and Germans and Swedish oblige by shipping to fill our auto backlog order for us. So when the strike is over, not as many auto workers are called back as before the strike.

And the foreign auto makers have a seller's market during the strike. So they raise prices. Inflation.

The Teamsters get their raise. It is partly wiped out immediately by the rising prices.

Other shortages have developed as well because of layoffs all along the line. Productivity goes to hell. Other prices rise. Everybody else now needs a raise. "The truckers got theirs. We have to go after ours." More strikes. More shortages. More inflation.

Productivity is down the tubes.

Should strikes be outlawed? No, not in private industry.

Just as a manufacturer should have the right to withhold his product from market, the workingman must always have the freedom to withhold his labor.

But, just as there can be no preventing the customer from buying the product from another manufacturer, there should be no restricting the manufacturer's freedom to hire other workers if his regular people refuse to work.

The right to strike, yes. . .but no right to prevent anyone else from doing the work.

I must have my freedom to strike, but you must be free not to buy my food for me or pay my rent if I make that decision.

As it is now we subsidize the striker: food stamps, welfare payments, and unemployment compensation.

That makes us pay not once but twice for a decision made by the striker in which we had no voice. We pay once in the benefits for the striker off work, a second time because the strike raises prices we pay.

We must have the freedom to strike. But if we don't find a way to voluntarily end major strikes, we are going to destroy our productivity and purchasing power. How do we do that? We'll get to that later.

But some strike action needs to be outlawed. The laws are

already on the books but union leadership is officially and unofficially exempt.

Strong-arm tactics must be just as illegal for unions as for any other citizen.

Beyond that, unions should be held to the same laws as the rest of us. Right now they are exempt from antitrust laws forbidding restraint of trade. Transportation unions restrain trade to the point where the International Longshoremen's and Warehousemen's Union a few years past shut down all West Coast trade for 131 days, causing untold havoc. The Maritime Union and the Teamsters base their whole strategy on being able to restrain trade. Airline pilots and controllers have tried to do the same.

But if you or I restrain trade, we are in trouble with the law.

Much union clout depends not upon the hardship they can inflict upon their employer, but how much they inflict upon the general citizenry so that we go in and fight their battles for them. Postal workers, police, firemen, rubbish men, government transit workers—all of them try to make the citizen holler "Uncle."

What everybody forgets is that these damaged citizens are also workers. Unions hurt workers...and unionized workers are only 20 percent of our working people.

The City Hall Syndrome. Government employee unions are now the fastest-growing organized labor segment. Membership in manufacturing unions has dropped a half million in a half decade; government employee union membership grew over a half million in two years.

And these unions have developed a highly effective strategy. When a brand-new city administration takes office after defeating a labor-wise, battle-scarred old incumbent, the city unions strike for a major raise.

The newcomer has promised to run the city efficiently. Ten minutes after he takes office, his city is plunged into labor chaos. Multiple services, which the outgoing mayor had under control, suddenly go out on strike. The new administration is confronted by highly experienced veteran union chiefs, totally professional. The new administration personnel are babes in these woods by comparison.

After a few weeks the new administration, desperate to salvage its "first hundred days," capitulates in an inflationary settlement.

Thus our public servants have become our bosses.

. . . and by assuming to themselves the powers of government may sweep away the liberties of the continent like a deluge.

—Common Sense

Unionized government employees so dominate some city halls and statehouses that they have brought many near bankruptcy, New York City being the classic example.

In at least a dozen states, unions have won the passage of laws under which government agencies force public employees to pay dues to unions to hold their jobs. How does government then operate to our advantage if its workers have two bosses, a well-organized union and an unorganized us?

Since the government employee is charged with our *security*—the only legitimate function of government—he should no more have the right to strike than a uniformed infantryman.

If the government employee is *not* essential to our security (broadly interpreted), we should not have him on staff anyway.

. . . here too is the design and end of government, viz., freedom and security.

—Common Sense

Does the government employee have the right to quit? Sure, after due notice. But he should not be allowed to leave his post all of a sudden anymore than the infantryman is.

Unionized government employees have demonstrated a cavalier disregard for citizen security. They prove out an observation of economists Milton and Rose Friedman: "The gains strong unions make for their workers are at the expense of other workers."

Nobody's money. The states are now finding out that binding arbitration with unionized government employees is not working, and courts are overturning statutes granting collective bargaining rights to state employees.

Compulsory bargaining has not improved government services; rather, it has worsened them. Government employees in general have long had the attitude that the money paid them is nobody's money. But it is. It's your tax money, levied to provide you specific services. Under unionization and compulsory bargaining, you as taxpayer buy even less productivity.

Wisconsin was the first state to extend compulsory bargaining to the public sector. The year before it did this in 1958, there were 15 government strikes nationwide involving 1,730 employees and a loss of 7,520 workdays. In 1975, with similiar government employee laws and unionization in thirty-four states, there were 478 strikes involving 318,000 employees and a loss of 2,204,000 workdays.

The arbitrators in every settlement gave practically no attention to the ability to pay of the states and cities.

Many governments are now considering abandoning collective bargaining for public employees; some are considering outlawing it.

When government salaries trailed other salaries, there was a kind of tradition of dedication to the public service. Paradoxically, now that government salaries *lead* the other sectors, there is a growing tradition of "the public be damned."

End wasteful strikes. The destructive effect of strikes on all of us is clear.

It is equally clear that a man's freedom to withhold his labor from the market—his only final resort against severe employment abuse—cannot be taken away from him in a free country (except for government employees).

While labor's recent excesses are acknowledged, management's similar excesses are proved history, and nothing guarantees against their recurrence if the pendulum swings again.

So how do we eliminate strikes?

We probably don't eliminate them totally. But what lies within our capability is to reduce them:

1. Eliminate public tax relief of the strikers so that the workman, before he votes for a strike, knows that he, not his neighbor, bears the burden.
2. Overturn legislation preventing the employer from hiring a substitute for the man who elects to walk off the job.
3. Provide retraining loans for a worker whose job is eliminated by technology.

Two parts of the problem remain beyond our present capability, because Gus Kish doesn't believe. Those two are:

1. There is as yet no incentive for union leadership to take the risk of choosing a sound but unpopular course—favoring increased buying power over increased paper dollars in the pay envelope.
2. There is no incentive as yet for the management man in a labor dispute to take a prudent position that will benefit the company over the long range after he's gone but which will make him look bad to the stockholders over a short range.

That is the unresolved challenge to management and labor leadership.

The most notable experiment thus far. In 1973, the steel companies under the chief industry negotiator and the USW under I.W. Abel got together to try an experiment. They wanted to break up a vicious cycle. That three-year cycle was this:

1. Customer stockpiling in anticipation of strike at negotiation time
2. Strike
3. Settlement
4. Fewer workers recalled because of customer stockpiling and customers lost to foreign suppliers.

To avert the usual strike in 1973, tremendous preparatory indoctrination of rank and file on the consequences of a strike preceded negotiations, which were called "experimental negotiations." Both parties agreed to employ and abide by the decision of an arbitrator on any points they could not resolve.

On one hand, the experimental plan worked. There was no strike in 1973, nor in 1977, or 1980. On the other hand, the extravagant pay gains made by the workmen under this plan brought the industry to a very dangerous condition.

No. 3: Unwittingly Unions Become Anti-Worker

Everybody knows unions righted awesome wrongs. There's no argument on that point. But few realize the pendulum has swung so far back that unions now hurt workers. Whenever a union gains the majority of employees in a plant, it becomes the exclusive bargaining agent for all employees, including those who prefer to bargain for themselves or prefer to have a different representative of their own choosing. The law forbids the employer from bargaining with any other agent or with the individual employee.

This monopoly climate spawns raw power.

This heavy political and economic clout is used not only on the union's own members, it also brings political candidates into the union corner and thus in a sense the union into our government.

We could point to dangers in that perhaps, but the way in which the union has most damaged the worker is by leading him into a suicidal sequence of unearned raises.

Super-high labor costs prevent us from competing in world markets, leading directly to unemployment at home as we have sent our greatest industries overseas: textiles, home appliances, sporting goods, bicycles, motorcycles, autos, and steel.

This unemployment has led in sure-fire sequence to massive welfarism, which has led to huge deficit spending with directly rocketing inflation.

The thoughtful economist, Henry Hazlitt, concludes after a lifetime of study:

> *The net overall effect of union policy has been to reduce productivity, to discourage new investment, to slow down capital formation, to distort the structure and balance of production, to drive non-union members into lower paid jobs and to reduce the total production and total real wages and real income for the whole body of workers below what it otherwise would have been. The public must recognize that the interests of union leaders are by no means identical with the interests of labor as a whole, and that being pro-union is by no means synonymous with being pro-labor.*[2]

No. 4: Unions Originally Restricted Employment...and Some Still Do.

Before we get our hackles up over that, it is well to look at history prior to the arrival on the scene of labor heroes like Gompers and Lewis and Green. A startling view is presented by Milton and Rose Friedman. They remind us that the first objective of unionism was *not* the elevation of the rank and file, but *exclusion* of them. Limit the number of people employed in the

2. From *Conquest of Poverty,* p. 141.

field. The Friedmans feel that the first union was probably the doctors, leagued under that much revered Code of Hippocrates. That code had an ugly side not framed in doctors' offices. It said in effect, "*I agree not to teach healing to others, except for my sons and the sons of other healers.*"

The Friedmans point out that today those who pressure for licensing and for higher minimum wages are not poor people, but union lobbyists protecting union members from competition. Minimum wage laws require the employer to discriminate against the low skill people just as doctors' fees remain high by limiting the supply of doctors.

Samuel Gompers said, "Labor's objective is *more!*"

No. 5: Government Help for Workers Boomerangs Against Workers

Labor's huge ally, big government, hurts workers.

The government has just chopped off the starting rungs of the career ladder.

We all need some way to get a foot on a bottom rung, some place to start, some place where we can learn an industry and a career.

The government, in its massive callousness, has wiped out the career starting place for our youth and, in the same stroke, institutionalized another welfare generation.

Walter Williams is a whip-figured bright black man, up from the slums of Philadelphia the hard way. He drifted around as a young man trying to get ahead and finally decided he needed an education. He worked his way to a doctorate in economics in the days before the government was helping blacks do that. It took him ten years, but when he got through he had some important ideas about what was holding young people down. He has in fact become a nationally recognized expert on that issue, and dozens of committees of Congress are constantly asking him to educate them on that subject.

He gets very depressed about increases in the federal minimum wage. "That guarantees maximum unemployment for the young and unskilled, particularly blacks." Williams sees recent minimum wage increases as increasing black youth unemployment 35 percent to 40 percent. "How else do you explain the massive change from waiter service to self-service in restaurants?"

"How else do you explain the sudden absence of ushers in movies and the absence of youngsters at supermarkets to take your bags to the car? We have cut the bottom rungs off the economic ladder, and (thus) developed a permanent welfare class.

"Child labor laws in the thirties protected youth from working in cold dangerous mines. But today these same laws protect young people from working in air-conditioned offices. *Why is it better for a young man to be unemployed at $3.20 an hour than employed at $2.00?*"

Williams is also appalled that over six hundred occupations require licenses. "In some states you need a license to be a beauty operator or a landscaper. Our founding fathers thought that a man had a right to practice a trade without going to the feudal lord to get permission. But we have built the same system our founding fathers sought to escape.

"In sum, the government has passed many laws designed to help the lowest skilled worker but has actually hurt him."

What is required is explained by Williams, "Black people do not need any special programs. All they need is for the government to get off their backs."

No. 6: When Labor Decides to Run a Business Successfully, Labor Runs It the Way Business Runs a Business

Aeroquip Corporation of Youngstown, Ohio, a subsidiary of Libbey-Owens-Ford, was doing poorly in 1978 and was going to be shut down. The company made rubber hydraulic hose.

Youngstown had already experienced disastrous shutdowns in the steel industry. There weren't going to be other jobs available for those laid off. Frank Ciarniello, a machine operator and head of the United Rubber Workers local in the plant, went to management and asked if the employees could buy the business before they shut it down.

Management said yes. . . if the employees could raise the $2.5 million price.

They did and immediately set out to make the failing plant profitable.

How did they do it?

Workers basically understand the common sense of business. So when they are running their *own* plant, they run it differently than they talk at the bargaining table to corporate management.

First move: They cut the number of salaried employees from fifty to sixteen. Second move: They cut hourly wages from $6.60 per hour to $5.00. Third move: They cut paid holidays from twelve to eight. Fourth move: They reduced five-week vacations to three weeks and for the first year allowed no vacations, period. Fifth move: They axed the costly pension plan, which had been eating $1 million a year, 7 percent of the operating budget.

When union men take over a business to make it work, they do what a good business management does.

Wherefore, instead of gazing at each other with suspicious or doubtful curiosity, let each of us hold out to his neighbor the hearty hand of friendship and unite in drawing a line which, like an act of oblivion, shall bury in forgetfulness every former dissension.

—Common Sense

No. 7: When Labor and Management Are Allowed to Work Together in Common Sense Ways Rather than Through Lawyers, Miracles Happen

The truth provides a challenge to management and labor leadership: Workers know more about running a business than the usual restrictive relationship allows them to contribute. Can you take advantage of that?

The "restrictive relationship" includes union restrictions, legal restrictions, peer pressure, and a cultivated adversarial relationship.

If you can dump that, you can lick the world.

The Tarrytown turnaround. The big Chevrolet plant in Tarrytown, New York, had the reputation of the lowest quality and worst labor relations record of all General Motors operations. At this writing, it has the reputation of the best.

The turnaround came quickly and began the moment Tarrytown management and workers became convinced that Detroit management was about to shut the plant down. The record was dismal: 7 percent absenteeism, 2,000 backlogged grievances. Shop chairman Larry Sheridan said, "The plant was a battleground."

In desperation, Tarrytown began an experiment based on the

idea that the men on the line probably knew more about how to improve quality and performance than they let on. Why not use all the shop floor expertise?

It is not in numbers but in unity that our great strength lies.
—Common Sense

A new mood began with model changeover. Tarrytown management showed workers proposed changes in the assembly line and invited comments.

"A lot of good ideas came forward," said Gus Beirne, shop superintendent. "Things we'd missed; and we had time to correct."

The cost savings were impressive, so they went a step further, regular meetings with plant people.

In the windshield installation department, a bad quality complaint area, they discovered that among the thirty installers each selected a different point around the windshield to start applying the sealant. But one man explained that he began at the point where the radio antenna wires came out of the glass, "because you get a little extra adhesive, a puddle that stops leaks."

When that method was adopted, dealer complaints about windshield leaks dropped to zero.

Management moved next to the welders. Within months bad welds dropped from 35 percent to 1.5 percent.

"The evolution that has taken place in this plant is terrific," explains Ray Calore, president of the local U.A.W. "No more hidden ball tricks."

Absenteeism dropped from 7 percent to 2.5 percent, and there are only thirty grievances backlogged.

Three thousand jobs that were definitely going to be lost by eroding productivity were saved.

No. 8: Labor Owns Business

Someday labor is in for the surprise of its life. Probably too late. It has not discovered that it *owns* the great industrial golden goose that it threatens to kill.

Labor is still sitting on the sidelines cheering on government, urging it to clobber industry's attempt to form the capital to buy new and more productive machines. Labor applauds when government forces industry to dissipate capital into all kinds of nonproductive equipment and programs. Labor acts as if that is not their fight. Yet, strangely, it is more labor's fight than anyone's. Labor leadership does not warn its members of the hazard in 10 percent raises when productivity increases only 1.1 percent and in many cases actually decreases.

That is probably because the working man has not yet learned that labor owns voting control of many of the top 1,000 corporations via its pension funds. They have the most to lose by the death of free enterprise capitalism, namely their pensions.

The power of the pension funds is not a secret to the union leadership; but the few union leaders who are using that power tend to use it suicidally.

Pension funds carry tremendous clout. With $550 billion in assets, these pension funds hold more than 25 percent of all publicly traded stock, and are the dominant source of industry's outside capital.

A few union leaders wish to use their stockholder voting rights (from invested pension funds) to coerce companies into unprofitable moves such as heavier social benefit programs—health, housing, day-care, environmental equipment, extreme safety expenditures—than the companies can profitably carry.

But there is a perfect way to use the pension power. Use that power to push for profit sharing. Roger B. Smith, chairman of General Motors, indicates, "Now is the time for profit sharing." With a profit-sharing plan in place, both management and labor have the incentive to pull in the same direction.

Adversarial attitudes diminish. Creative initiative and cooperation are released to produce Sam Gompers' one word objective for all—*more*.

Maybe you agree—that what we need to reach Sam Gompers' goal is to give ourselves a raise via a sounder dollar?

And we don't need fancy statistical reports to know when we achieve that. All we need to do to see what progress we are making is to monitor our weekly market baskets. Then, once a month, we can ask our post office, "How many dollars needed to buy a gold medallion today?"

If it takes fewer dollars for either of these, *we have our raise.*

And that is the best kept secret of more take-home pay.

3

MORE INDEPENDENCE—
LESS WELFARE

Welfare makes people poor.
And keeps them poor.
And makes their children poor.
And makes their nation poor.

Two Women

Susan. Monday morning the employment agent received a phone call from the personnel director of Foote, Cone & Belding, a large Chicago advertising agency, "Where's Susan?"

Remember Susan from Chapter 1? The agent had worked especially hard to get Sue this chance to start work. It required good agentry because Susan, twenty-two, had no work skills; no work record. She had a two-year-old child and no husband. She had been on welfare all her adult life. However, she had arranged for her sister to care for the baby while she went to work.

The agent had persuaded the employer to give Susan training after she had been on the job for six months. She would get a 10 percent raise at six months, another at twelve months.

The agent anxiously dialed Susan, "How come you're home? Why didn't you go to work?"

"My welfare counselor advised me I would be better off not to take the job—better off with my welfare payments."

True. The sum of Susan's ADC payments, food stamps, and

rent supplement was a small net gain over her starting salary, because for work she would have to pay carfare and buy clothes.

But the job at Foote, Cone & Belding promised professional training, raises, and a foot on the career ladder.

Most of all, it promised pride and freedom.

Instead, the welfare counselor had kept Susan poor probably for life.

Ye that oppose independence now, ye know not what ye do; ye are opening a door to eternal tyranny.

—Common Sense

Welfare is cruel.

Begun out of kindness, it now locks people into the kind of feudalistic poverty and dependence men fought a thousand years to escape. By diverting people from the career starting place, the so-called lowly jobs, the welfare state deflects them forever from their chance at the brass ring and economic freedom. Their children, with no model of a working parent, drift right into what they are taught—career welfare.

Jodi Almendariz. According to the May 1980 issue of *Quest*, "She was well on her way to a lifetime of failure." At twenty-eight, she had dropped out of San Antonio High and four marriages, "and seemed destined to permanent dependence upon welfare." Defeat was already in her slump-shouldered, aimless gait.

However, she encountered a soft-spoken lady named Lupe Anguiano, who had a questing sadness in her eyes and had started a group she dubbed National Women's Employment and Education, Incorporated, a nonprofit corporation.

"The effect of welfare," says Lupe Anguiano, "is to keep women under the poverty level. It *should* get them *off* welfare." Ms. Anguiano is a handsome dark-haired woman who quit the government's Women's Action Program of the then Department of Health, Education and Welfare to start her nongovernment group.

She launched NWEE in an empty store front with the slogan "Let's Get Off Welfare!"

In thirty days she shows a woman how to reinterpret her past experience as possible qualification for some kind of work, how to handle job interviews, how to dress for them. Then she sends some of the women to free high school adult education classes.

"The women hate welfare," Lupe says, "so they study harder than most people, and more eagerly."

Lupe then finds the women jobs, preferably with companies that run at least a small training program. In her first two years, Lupe placed 408 welfare women in regular jobs. Only 42 of these lost their jobs and returned to welfare. Net victories in just those two years: 366 women free of welfare.

It probably also means their children will be off welfare. That's important.

Lupe Anguiano placed these women at an average cost of $671 per woman, using privately raised funds. The government's CETA program averages $4,000 per placement, and CETA uses three-months retention of job as the criterion in counting its victories. Lupe uses one year. Her first year's batting average was .800.

So what about Jodi Almendariz, high school dropout, four times divorced? Lupe sent her to free high school adult education classes for three months, then landed her a job operating a back hoe for a Texas construction company.

Ms. Almendariz says there is no chance "I will ever be on welfare again. If I lost this job, with what I know now, I'd have another job," she whips off a gauntlet and snaps her fingers, "like that."

More impressive than the big dollars is Jodi Almendariz's posture—straight and tall.

Government Welfare Helps the Wrong People.

On the one hand is Tyrone Robinson. At 2:00 P.M., June 13, 1980, with a silver crucifix around his neck, Robinson, thirty-one years old and a paraplegic, drove his seven-year-old Buick Electra through the street crowd celebrating the Downtown Cleveland festival and straight up the granite steps of City Hall, a block from the country welfare office.

He was stone sober.

Outraged city officials, quickly surrounding the car, calmed down when they saw Robinson was even more outraged than they were. They thought he might be dangerous.

"Why do you only listen to me when I drive up the steps?"

he asked them. "Why can't you do what you're supposed to do? I want some action not just for me...but all paraplegics."

Robinson, who had been crippled by a gunshot in 1973, had been promised employment with a federal jobs program by city officials.

For months he had propelled his wheelchair from door to door in welfare corridors, getting only talk and papers to fill out. Now he was broke and could not support his family. Welfare offices routed him through another paperwork maze with desultory attention...until, in despair, he drove his Buick up City Hall steps.

On the opposite hand, Ms. Alheim, a student at Vassar, received a startling invitation letter from her government. She is the daughter of Richard A. Alheim, president of a substantial Rochester firm supplying industrial hardware and a very astute businessman with successful investments. So Ms. Alheim was surprised at the letter from her government, which she read to her father over the phone. He in turn phoned the authors of this volume in profane frustration. The letter informed Ms. Alheim that as a student she was officially at the poverty level and thus qualified to receive food stamps, for which she was encouraged to apply.

At about the same time Jim Zwerlein, attending college in the Upper Michigan Peninsula, wrote to his parents in Westlake, Ohio, as they were about to leave for their winter home in Florida, that he and a half dozen classmates had just bought filet mignon with their food stamps and were about to stage a cookout for their Saturday night dates.

And in this way, multiplied by tens of millions of absurdities, the great United States bastion of self-reliance and independence converted itself eagerly and with the help of its leaders into the world's largest welfare state.

The United States—Welfare State?

Everyone has heard of the common welfare programs; Aid to Dependent Children (ADC), food stamps, supplemental feeding, rent supplements, unemployment compensation. But few know that there are over one hundred federal welfare programs costing about $90 billion annually *over and above* the $130 billion annual Social Security payout. (These do not include state, county, and municipal welfare programs.)

These federal programs consumed $220 billion in one recent year, exceeding the entire 1970 federal budget. Yes, the United States is a welfare state.

Higher figures are quoted by some; we will use the conservative figures. They're big enough.

Devastating as the dollar cost may be, the far greater cost is to the character of the nation. Massive erosion of freedom, self-reliance, and honor has been the net result.

To (mis)administer that welfare monster requires a pervasive bureaucracy which now wields enormous authority over us, stripping away freedom of both the beneficiaries and the benefactors. The bureaucrats rule.

O ye that love mankind! Ye that dare oppose not only the tyranny but the tyrant, stand forth! Every spot of the Old World is overrun with oppression. Freedom has been hunted round the globe.

—Common Sense

The erosion of self-reliance is typified by Susan's decision against a job. With the counsel of our government employee, Susan chose career welfare.

The built-in incentive for dishonor is notorious.

Important amounts of the $220 billion giveaway are consumed by waste and fraud. The waste comes, as Milton and Rose Friedman explain, because *other* people are giving away still *other* people's money. The dishonor occurs because the incentive is incredibly huge and the funding so vast that fraud and waste cannot even be monitored.

Welfare superstars. The welfare queens have arrived. A Los Angeles woman received $240,000 over six years, based on her paper claims for sixty-six children she does not have. A Chicago graduate student received $150,000 in illegal welfare payments from 1972 to 1978. At that time already, HEW's own accountants blithely estimated $1 billion a year lost in ADC payments alone.

When state or county governments launch special crackdowns on welfare fraud and abuse, they find startling percentages of welfare recipients ineligible. The District of Columbia, for example, discovered 17 percent of recipients ineligible and 13 percent overpaid.

When local crackdowns are publicized, switchboards light up with frightened welfare clients asking to be removed from the rolls. Officials congratulate themselves for these results, but the haunting question is: How many thousands of others were neither caught nor discouraged?

Welfare festival. The citizen taxpayer feels quite foolish as he passes St. Clair Avenue and West Third Street in Cleveland on the days when county welfare checks are to be picked up there. In front of the building a mini-festival is in swing. Two colorful vendor umbrellas are surrounded by well-dressed welfare clients greeting each other familiarly and buying hot dogs, pop, stuffed animals, balloons, and whirligigs. St. Clair Avenue is clogged with double -parked, well-waxed Olds 98s, Thunderbirds, occasional Cadillacs, and Marks. These are not rusting junkers. Behind each wheel slouches a sharply dressed man waiting for his woman to come out of the building. At the request of policemen, these getaway drivers grudgingly start to move their cars, then settle back when the officer has passed.

This street fair is two blocks from the City Hall steps that Tyrone Robinson had to drive up in order to get some attention for a real need.

There is no question that we should and must take care of our hungry, injured, and poor. But $1 billion a year in just one program for mistakes, waste, and fraud?

Should we be supporting people like the man in Wisconsin with six dependents who turned down, in favor of welfare, a job paying $700 per month because this was less than his welfare payments? He can do that legally. Federal rules prohibit suspending state-administered federal welfare funds from able-bodied adults who refuse jobs paying less than their welfare grants.

This is common sense?

The Disaster Model
vs. Common Sense

If we were pioneering the welfare state, our mistakes could be forgiven. But models of welfare state failures are garishly available for easy study by our leaders.

They don't work.

What becomes visible slowly is that the *continuing* transfer of income from the producers to the nonproducers destroys the work incentive of *both*. Ultimately the producers stop producing.

England and Italy provided classic models of welfare state collapse. But then welfare enthusiasts pointed to the success of the Scandinavian and German welfare states.

Now, however, the Scandinavian welfare states are finding that, to support their tremendous welfare benefits, their diminishing productive output must be higher priced. They must then build protective tariffs shutting off the inflow of more favorably priced goods from outside—again raising costs—and 'round and 'round and down and down.

Are we digging our own grave? Martin Duyzing, writing in *To the Point,* December 1978, quotes an unnamed Englishman, "Perhaps this welfare state does take care of us from cradle to grave, the question is: Aren't we all busy digging our own grave?"

The Swedish worker, tiring of paying 70 percent taxes to his welfare state for cradle-to-grave protection, is now deciding that the only way to get some of it back is to queue up for state benefits he doesn't really need. According to the September 29, 1978, issue of *To the Point,* the workers of one whole department of the railway center of Hallsberg reported themselves sick for four months in order to draw sick pay. They didn't ask for a raise; they just wanted to "get some of it back" in the form of a vacation.

Swedes in mass numbers are coming up with scores of ingenious plans to draw more benefits as a way to "get some back"— to get *more*. Young couples abjure marriage so as to draw greater housing benefits as two single people. Students take college allowances and spend them for noncollege purposes.

New Zealand's welfare staters decided to do something nice for the single parent, a special substantial monetary allowance. When the decision was made, there were about 9,000 such single parents on record. Twelve months of this payment plan suddenly brought forward 28,000 new single parents. Couples actually separated to get the money.

Wherever the welfare state has existed, disaster has followed.

The model has been highly visible to our leaders. Despite congressional junkets to Europe, Congress has refused the lesson and put us on the same disaster track, on a larger scale.

It is a bobsled run straight into bondage.

Can You
Stop a Bobsled?

It will have to be *you,* the younger generation.

The seniors now in charge cannot do it.

Rendered helpless by welfarism, neither the leaders nor the recipients can cut it off as of some first of the month.

But a transitional move can be made, starting the transfer of millions out of dependency into independence. In just two years Lupe Anguiano transferred 408 out. This type of action, multiplied by thousands of such nongovernment operations, could remove millions of people from welfare.

Volunteerism could remove many from welfare rolls.

Those two methods merely prove that career welfarism can be licked. But the action must be stepped up by much more substantial efforts.

A comprehensive solution offering effective brakes for the bobsled has been proposed by the highly respected economists Rose and Milton Friedman. Their solution found its way into legislation but was so devastatingly amended and warped by the welfarists that the Friedmans had to lobby against it, and it was defeated. But it remains the most hopeful solution in sight.

The Friedman program would eliminate the staggering welfare bureaucracy by eliminating the hodge-podge of totally unadministratable specific welfare programs.

. . . that the more simple anything is, the less liable it is to be disordered and the easier repaired when disordered.
—Common Sense

The new program would not hand out milk, eyeglasses, food stamps, clothes allowances, summer camp vouchers, rent supplement tickets, hearing aids, and the myriad of specific earmarked grants.

It would give cash.

Let the recipient buy what he needs. Giving cash is also cheaper for the taxpayer.

What is this wonder program?

The Negative
Income Tax

The negative income tax concept could sweep away the thick catalog of welfare cruises and replace them all with one program, for which workable administrative machinery already exists.

How?

Under present income tax law we are allowed a certain amount of income free of tax. If your income is more than your allowances, you pay a tax on the overage, on an ascending scale.

So far, so good.

Now assume for a moment that my income is *less* than these allowances. Under the present system, I simply pay no income tax. But under negative income tax, I receive a subsidy proportional to the amount by which my income is *below* my allowances.

"What's the difference from welfare?" you ask. "Aren't you still going to sit on your duff and let me support you?"

No. Even If you give me no credit for human pride and dignity (and at this point, why should you?), I am still going to try to get a job, then a better job and even persuade the rest of my family to get jobs.

"Why would you? The less you earn, the more subsidy you get from me. The more you earn, the less you get from me."

True, but. . .the progressive percentage of my subsidy is set at such rates that my *total* income (my earnings plus the subsidy from you) is larger if I increase my *own* earnings.

"Okay. But that must mean there is some point in your earnings where you're better off to hang just below break-even, when you're not quite paying any taxes and you're still drawing a little subsidy from my taxes. You could just hang there forever, still a drag on the rest of us."

Probably not. If I'm doing that well I'm on the economic ladder. I'm better to climb on up, to get some promotions, pay some taxes, and be somebody.

But...for argument, let's say I have no pride. I'd rather hang just below break-even and get some subsidy. However, even so you, as taxpayer, are still so far ahead of where you are now that there is no comparison. You will have dumped an army of welfare bureaucrats and waste. And with the exception of prideless individuals like me, you will have motivated millions of people to be self-reliant.

The negative income tax gives help to the desperate in the form most useful to them—cash. And it is as automatic as a positive income tax. There's no begging for subsidy.

You would dump an army of bureaucrats because the negative income tax form of aid could and should be administered totally by the IRS. This would confine responsibility for administering aid to a single federal agency that already has the necessary machinery in place. Yes, administering negative income tax aid would increase the personnel at IRS by a few, but it would dismiss hordes from dozens of other bureaus at all levels of government.

"But what prevents you and many others from pressuring my congressman to increase the rate of cash subsidy you get from me?"

There is one additional step you should take: While I am receiving a subsidy from you, I should not be allowed to vote. It simply is not fair to let *me* vote to take money out of *your* pocket. As soon as I get off your subsidy, I should get my vote back.

"Won't you howl and scream about your constitutional rights being violated?"

Darn right. But for once in your life, you should be firm.

"What possible argument could I use?"

The most obvious in the world—do you know any other club in the world or union or organization that lets a member vote who does not pay his dues?

"Will that be enough of an arguement with 13 million voters on welfare?"

You have just answered your own question. If the subsidized voters can vote your income away from you increasingly, you will at some point elect to join me among the subsidized voters. When enough of you do this, whose income is left to support us?

The next step, inevitably, is that government must take over completely and order us to work.

Thoughtful men since Plato have known that democracy, with its right to vote, is delicate and vulnerable, having in it the seed of its own destruction. It is therefore essential to take away from the subsidized voter the key to his neighbor's corn crib. When he is ready to contribute some grain, he gets back the key immediately.

The one serious threat of the negative income tax is that, unless the recipients of negative income tax subsidy *lose* the vote, they would almost certainly be organized into a huge national Tammany Hall-type bloc that could destroy democracy, becoming a giant parasite sucking the life out of the nation.

With this negative income tax, all our deprived people can be served better than they are now, and millions of them will have financial and prideful incentive to climb off the welfare rolls to get their vote.

We will stop the bobsled ride into bankruptcy and bondage. And you will get me off your back.

"Not quite. I, the young taxpayer, will still probably have to pay about 10 percent of my earnings for your Social Security benefits. . . while you senior people paid a much smaller portion of your income into Social Security taxes."

That is true.

That's your next big job.

Social Security—
the Salesmanship
and
the Mythology

Social Security was the pivot that turned us.

Social Security was the first important switch in the track, diverting the whole fast freight into the welfare siding. And when the switch was thrown, it welded shut.

It was a sleeper.

Social Security, sold to the people and the congress as a *minimum safety net,* grew into a whole way of life. Meant as an emergency supplement to retirement plans, it became the whole plan.

We don't know that the 1933 Depression leadership can be blamed. Desperate men were seeking a solution to desperate times. Certainly the public can't be blamed for accepting it, considering the mythology used in selling it.

Up front, to quell alarm, note that any reasonable person knows the Social Security program cannot be canceled abruptly, but knows immediate action is necessary.

To advance freedom and improve the economy, a viable program should be substituted, without abrogating commitments to those who already have paid Social Security taxes.

Why a substitute?

Because the present Social Security is not workable finance. It is a series of myths piled on top of each other.

Myth number one: Social Security was sold to the public as *insurance* and is still called an *insurance* program. That left the citizen his pride. He was buying and paying for his own protection, an honorable, even shrewd and foresighted act. He was not accepting charity.

Fact: It is *not* an insurance program; never was.

Myth number two: The citizen's contributions would all go to form a giant trust fund which, when invested, would grow and cover the payouts.

Fact: There is no trust fund. There are no trustees. The citizen contributions do not grow. They shrink from inflation and bureaucratization; and they never have covered the payouts, which come from additional taxation.

Myth number three: The citizen's input is actually called a *contribution,* a word which elevated the citizen.

Fact: It is not a contribution. It is a tax, forcibly collected before the citizen even touches his pay.

Myth number four: The literature speaks of the *employer* contribution, implying cooperative sharing of the cost between employee and employer. This gives the program a nice aura of mutuality.

Fact: The employees pay the whole bill. The employer merely considers his Social Security tax as part of his labor cost and passes that cost on, like any cost, by raising prices as a hidden sales tax. Or he reduces his number of employees accordingly, just as he does when forced to pay a raise he cannot afford. Under Social Security, he must use fewer employees.

These misconceptions were supportable up to the time when payouts so far outran Social Security revenues that the augmentation money from the general fund could no longer be hidden. Now we can all see that there will soon not be enough worker taxpayers to support the receivers of the checks.

It is common sense that a new system must be substituted before Social Security destroys itself and us. That new system, common sense dictates, must be fair to all. The gross inequities of Social Security will not allow it to stand without bitterly dividing us.

Promoters of Social Security have told us that we would each draw out in proportion as we paid in. But in reality benefits drawn out have a poor correlation to the amount paid in by the beneficiary. For example, a widow who did not pay into the system but gets the widow's benefit from her husband's Social Security tax payments receives the same amount as a widow who worked and paid into the system and whose husband also paid Social Security taxes.

A woman over sixty-five who continues to work full-time does not receive any Social Security benefit. In fact she must continue to pay Social Security taxes for the benefit of the lady who quit working or never did pay Social Security.

A young man from a low income family generally starts work earlier in life than a wealthy one who goes to college and graduate school; hence he starts paying in earlier. He probably works longer and dies younger, drawing fewer retirement checks than the wealthy lad who pays in less and draws out more.

The first Social Security retiree began drawing benefits on January 1, 1940, after paying in only $22.54 in payroll taxes. Upon her death, she had drawn $21,000 in retirement payments.

Before the system ever had a chance to catch up and get on a self-financing basis, new groups of people who had not been paying into the system were brought under the Social Security umbrella by congressional act.

For example, in 1952, self-employed people were allowed to come in. Self-employers, then approaching retirement were allowed to pay $121.50 in Social Security taxes in eighteen months. They retired with $80 monthly pensions.

Those who did that and are still living are now receiving $179 per month. Such citizens have now drawn $47,000 apiece, not counting any dependent or survivor benefits. These massive unearned benefit payouts put the system billions of dollars behind its income. Payouts have had to come from the general fund.

Thirty-five million people (retirees, disabled workers, adult survivor dependents, and children survivor dependents) are now drawing benefits. Supporting those 35 million via payroll taxes are 110.5 million. We are approaching a ratio of three workers supporting one beneficiary.

A 1950 Senate and House Committee recommendation for Social Security revisions forecast that in fifty years estimated annual payouts would be nearly $12 billion. The forecast was low. Social Security payout already exceeds $130 billion.

Although the 1977 tax increases for Social Security were the largest peacetime tax increases in our history, weekly statements from Social Security administrators still predict expiration of retirement payment resources before the next programmed tax increase.[1]

The number of people receiving benefits is growing faster than the number of providers. As we've just noted, already three of us work to support one. And any stutter in the the economy worsens that ratio.

Unforeseen or ignored by legislators writing Social Security law are disaster "built-ins." In 1972, for example, we hooked an automatic cost-of-living raise to Social Security benefit payments. Edward Graunlich, a senior fellow at Brookings Institution, assumed a continuing inflation rate equal to that existing in 1975 and extended the figures forward to year 2045. He concluded that under existing laws, a median wage worker living with spouse in year 2045 would be eligible to collect 173 percent of his preretirement wage, tax free, in the first year of his retire-

1. Yes, you've seen Social Security tax increases several times since 1977, but these were built into that year's law. The law provided for an increase to 6.05% of income for salaried workers in 1978; to rise to 6.13% in 1980, to 6.65% in 1981, to 6.7% in 1982, and to 7% in 1985. There has also been a series of increases in the base annual salary subject to this tax. The self-employed worker at this point must pay close to 10% of income remaining after deduction of allowable business expenses.

ment. That would require a payroll tax rate on the working population of 40 percent.

And by a plain method of argument, as we are running the next generation into debt, we ought to do the work of it; otherwise we use them meanly and pitifully.

—Common Sense

The commitment to present and future beneficiaries already paying into the system reaches into the trillions.

This is not workable.

Yet it is politically infeasible to abort the system.

Unhooking;
but Not Cold Turkey

The Social Security welfare drug, which hooked many Americans on not providing for themselves individually, cannot be quit abruptly. But we must quit it if we are to survive as a healthy, prosperous nation.

Of the plans offered for unhooking America, Milton Friedman's comprehensive plan is again the most practical we have reviewed, and the withdrawal pains will not kill the addict.

First, *terminate existing Social Security taxes.*

Convert Social Security to private retirement and security plans immediately. The objectives would be essentially the same as the Social Security objectives but would include strong tax incentives to encourage maximum participation by the citizen. The operation would be similar to the present government-approved Keogh and IRA (Individual Retirement Account) plans.

Second, *continue to pay beneficiaries under Social Security according to present law.* A self-respecting nation must pay its debts. When the old plan is replaced by a new plan, the Social Security obligations existing at that time must still be paid. And payments should increase or decrease with consumer prices, as they do now. Tax revenue must be made to cover this by reducing other expenses and not be increasing debt or taxes. That will avoid further inflation.

Third, *honor the future Social Security claims that tax payments thus far have earned.*

Fourth, *to the worker who has not yet earned full coverage, give government bonds equal to the payroll taxes he and his employer have paid in for him.*

Fifth, *stop the further build-up of benefits,* letting each worker use the saved tax money he will not now pay to invest for his own future in a private retirement plan.

This transition does not commit the government to further blank-check debts. It ends open-end promises. The benefit is compounded by relief from the costs of the Social Security bureaucracy, which would be demobilized.

This plan puts in broad daylight the kind of obligations now concealed. It funds pensions that will be earned in the future.

Allowable deductions for individual retirement plans should be expanded to be made more attractive.

A 20/20 Plan

A 20/20 plan would let citizens look out for their own future. Up to 20 percent of personal income would be allowed deductible for insurance premiums plus 20 percent of the cost of those premiums. This would make total IRS-allowable deductions equal 120 percent of the retirement insurance paid, giving the citizen strong incentive for maximum individual saving for future security.

This increased federal income tax deduction seems reasonable, since the huge cost of government administration of Social Security would be eliminated. Administration costs would shift to private insurance companies.

Private pension companies competing for the business would quickly offer a variety of attractive pension and disability insurance plans. These would not entail the expensive Social Security bureaucracy itself soaking up the money.

The 20/20 plan should be offered by private insurance companies approved and guaranteed by a government agency similar to FDIC (Federal Deposit Insurance Corporation).

Won't that add some more tax-absorbent bureaucracy? No. FDIC is self-supporting, funded by the industry it oversees.

However, no plan will safeguard a person's future—and that includes any variant on Social Security—unless the melting of the value of our dollar is halted and gradually reversed. Anything else is false security.

The most cruel act of negligence on the part of government has been to pull the sound dollar out from under the aging person's retirement plan when it is too late for him to build his own plan. We saw what that did to C.J. Meiggs' plan. It ended in a garage sale.

Absence of Social Security's depressant effect on working and hiring would result in higher national income. It would incite savings, which would create more capital, stimulating a more rapid growth in national income.

But what about the truly unfortunate person who has no retirement income? Shall we just leave him to the wolves?

No. He would receive major support from the federal negative income tax, remember?

There should be no federal unemployment insurance program. It is already clear from reports from the General Accounting Office that this has become emphatically a work disincentive program. It has reached the status of an on-going handout instead of emergency relief. Unemployment insurance is not an appropriate federal activity for taxpayers to carry on their backs.

But what about situations of extreme and disastrous unemployment, as witnessed in late 1982, when caravans of northern families, their unemployment benefits exhausted, migrated to Texas oil country only to find no jobs? Tent cities, soup kitchens, suicides resulted.

Nothing for them? No help?

Big help—the negative income tax. It works automatically and fast.

Artificial government job programs require months of legislation and months of organization, and then they don't apply to everyone who needs work. They are poor support for a family needing food and rent money *this week*.

Negative income tax would have quick reaction time and would apply to *every* family in catastrophic need, not just those who could get to a job program or learn about it or qualify for it.

The negative income tax will relieve extreme hardship—do it more economically, do it fairly, and do it quickly.

Additionally, it will decrease the severity of economic fluctuations and build towards a recovery that can be sustained.

Government Medicine

The following patients are not to be resuscitated: very elderly, over 65 years old, malignant disease, chronic chest disease, chronic renal.

That is government medicine.

That directive was posted on the bulletin board of Neasden Hospital, London. Ethel Morse, guest columnist in the April 6, 1979, issue of *The Naples Star* (Florida), explains that the directive "further instructed that if the hearts of the above categories of people stopped, they should not be revived by open chest massage and electrical stimulation."

This is government medicine.

Do we want it?

Mrs. Morse's study of socialized medicine finds it a disaster in all the socialist and communist countries. It leads to defective and inadequate hospitals. She cites a surgeon at London's Fulham Hospital who charges that 90 percent of British hospitals are so out of date that surgeons must operate in temperatures above 80 degrees along with 90 percent humidity and no ventilation; some patients suffer heat stroke.

Medical News, October 21, 1974, reported that 27 percent of all known food poisoning in England occurred in hospitals. Being government-owned, they are exempt from public health inspection.

Government medicine has led to a great emigration of doctors from England and a drastic deterioration in service. One-third of British medical graduates leave the nation.

A woman in Wales needing heart surgery had to wait six months for her appointment, then found the government bureaucracy had cancelled her appointment. She died two days later. A man in Britain needing surgery after a motor car accident was in pain and unable to work. He waited eleven months for surgery. A woman went to the hospital for a biopsy but had to wait two months. Then when the stitches were removed, she was advised the lump was malignant, but they could give her no firm date for surgery.

The chairman of the medical staff of two large hospitals in Bournemouth, England, complained of crowding so bad that patients who might have lived died while awaiting admission or died in the emergency room after waiting hours for a bed.

Another edition of *Medical News* charged that nearly 600,000 sufferers in Britain were being forced to wait for elective surgery to relieve their suffering.

Sweden's vaunted government medicine also builds backlogs. "Patients wait seven years for plastic surgery, three years for gall bladder, five for varicose vein surgery, two years for eye and ear clinic appointments." Swedes cannot choose their own doctors, and many of them are treated by a different doctor each time. The doctors do not have control over their assignments.

When socialized medicine came to England, the following events occurred between 1965 and 1973: Hospital staffs increased 28 percent; administrative and clerical staffs increased 52 percent . But medical services delivered (measured by average number of daily occupied hospital beds) dropped 11 percent.

Every nation that has adopted socialized medicine has experienced debilitating deterioration of service within fifteen years.

Since we have had a chance to observe the working models of socialized medicine, is it common sense to follow the example?

Certainly we need improvement in our own system. Rocketing medical costs have left many vulnerable.

That problem must be solved.

But it is common sense *not* to give up the three great advantages of our system:

- competition between doctors in a system where the patient has *choice*.
- the American patient is the customer, the boss, and has the final say-so, whether poor or rich.
- freedom from government having any say-so about our bodies.

When government gets into anything, tyranny, inefficiency, and corruption follow. While that is bad in any sphere, in matters of health and life it is the ultimate tyranny, to be avoided at all cost.

Already, as reported to a House Subcommittee by Francis M.

Mullen, Jr., assistant director of the FBI's criminal investigation division, "The methods to commit fraud in the Medicare-Medicaid programs are virtually unlimited." He cited egregious case histories similar to one in which a single physician collected $2 million in two years from government-funded health care programs for the needy and elderly.

But if the government should stay out of medicine, how are the needy to be served?

Again, via the negative income tax, which leaves the low income citizen with his dignity and a cash subsidy so that he walks into the medical establishment as a customer, not supplicant.

Yes, even with that subsidy there will be cases where that will not be enough. Certainly as a nation we can supply special grants for such needy citizens without locking the whole population into a socialized medicine tyranny.

Individual concern for each other will do a lot of that. In addition to the 20/20 program for retirements, another 20/20 program for charitable giving should be available for those desiring to give assistance to IRS-approved charities, again moving a service from the government to a private sector.

Private insurance companies competing in open market will do more toward providing health insurance for all levels of the population than any government.

The medical profession itself, despite its aggressive pricing, has a great record of individual doctors' medical philanthropy. In many communities peer pressure practically forces large-scale charitable medical practice.

Under socialized medicine, all this ends.

Volunteerism. In nearly every city and town, citizen volunteers organize to care for large numbers of financially troubled patients. Even among case-hardened cynics, the physical troubles of our neighbors tend to bring out our best side.

The potential of volunteerism is massive and ignored. If given real incentive, it could mushroom. It could return our freedom.

The Wall Street Journal's Michael Waldholz reports a great example: A nineteen-year-old stabbing victim is lying in a Bronx slum, critically wounded. Two ambulances arrive almost simultaneously. Two official city medics rush out of one ambulance. Out of the other emerge three hippies.

The city medics back off from the serious wound. They must send for more skilled help.

The hippies take charge. The young woman in jeans and an old bomber jacket binds up the man's intestines, which protrude from the wound. She instructs the city medic. A follow-up report states that this quick work saved the man's life. The police detective who called the hippies after waiting twenty minutes for the city ambulance was Timothy Bartlett. He said the hippies "put the city guys to shame."

These hippies are part of a thirty-five-member commune named Plenty. It is based in the South Bronx, and operates an ambulance service for the 600,000 people crowded into this twenty square miles of sometime misery.

Plenty is twelve men, eight women, and 15 children. Their mission is emergency aid for this area officially classified as "medically deprived."

Gary Spinner, bushy bearded with red hair tied back in braids, is the quiet, confident leader of the commune working in this hostile environment with great competence. "It's apparent the government isn't doing the job that's needed, and this community can't do it alone," he says.

Government has promised this slum area much and delivered little. Plenty promised nothing and "It's unimaginable how much they've done here," says Carolyn Gould, a health coordinator. "They're not like some razzle dazzle liberals. They've worked quietly and slowly to make themselves accepted."

You may say, "That's fine, but just a drop in the bucket. Volunteerism can't handle the volume." But consider this. Plenty's plan is to leave an experienced unit here in the Bronx, then move on to start a new one elsewhere.

Consider this also. Plenty is only a spinoff from a much larger commune in Tennessee called The Farm. It operates 1,750 acres for support of its 1,500 members and, in addition to other activities, operates an ambulance serving the poverty area of Tennessee.

The Farm sends members to troubled places as far away as Haiti and Bangladesh. It proves that volunteerism can come up with the troops to do the job.

In nearly every city and town, citizen volunteers organize to care for large numbers of financially troubled patients. Specialized volunteer groups organize to care for the crippled, blind, deaf, and severe arthritis sufferers. Volunteers care for terminal cancer patients who are without funds or family.

If we the authors found ourselves in such straits, we would rather be in the hands of a tender if untrained volunteer than at the mercy of a trained professional bureaucrat who would dictate the directive "The following patients are not to be resuscitated. . . ." We would rather die in good volunteer company than live in a bed ruled by a skilled tyrant.

Tom Paine told the colonies the same thing.

Patrick Henry told the burgesses.

Nathan Hale told the British.

The Huguenots told Europe.

Thousands of Cubans told Castro.

Hell—it's common sense.

4

MORE COMMON SENSE
—LESS REGULATION

ULTRA SECRET

TO: General Officers Only

For Electronic Decoding Only By Key 6849*SV-9

The essence of our attack strategy for the destruction of our enemy, the United States, will be to exercise every caution not to destroy its governmental regulatory bodies, neither at federal nor state levels. Deception attacks are encouraged to appear aimed at American governments; but in no case may an American governmental installation be significantly damaged by any commander, on pain of court martial.

The attack on the United States will employ the strategy of jujitsu, allowing the opponent's natural momentum to defeat itself.

Of several attack plans for destroying the United States, this is the most cost-effective strategy with minimum bloodshed and the best chance of not arousing the tremendous defense mechanism of the United States.

The plan prevents mobilization of the enemy's best strengths, destroys its productive power, demoralizes its people, and neutralizes the creative initiative of its population.

The imperative is to exercise all caution not to destroy its government. Let it continue to function and proliferate.

> *By Order,*
> *Commander-in-Chief*
> *All Forces Opposing the USA*

The U.S. vs. Us

The U.S. Department of Labor was about to put out of work some Vermonters who liked their work.

Susan Walsh, twenty-four, needed to work at home so she could watch the kids, Erin and Kerry. She knitted ski caps, which she sold to CB Sports, Inc., that way earning about $72.00 a week. She owned her own portable knitting machine and considered herself an independent businesswoman.

No, decided Herbert Cohen from the Labor Department. She was really an underpaid employee of CB Sports, Inc. and, as such, she must work in the factory. CB Sports, Inc. had a factory set among dairy farms and rural beauty along the Appalachian Trail.

But Mrs. Walsh couldn't leave home and the kids. So, if Mr. Cohen from Washington had his way, a lot of women like Mrs. Walsh could not knit ski caps at home. He said the purpose of the 1938 law that he was going to enforce was to eliminate the abuses of sweatshops. What it threatened to do in Vermont was eliminate a fine cottage industry.

This is common sense?

Cecile Duffany, a fifty-eight-year-old invalid who liked being self-reliant, also knitted ski caps at home, earning about $50.00 a week, plus some more for watching the children of some women who do go to the CB Sports factory to make ski parkas.

She resented Cohen's "protection." "The government should keep its nose out of it."

"No," disagreed Mr. Cohen. *"It's our experience that it doesn't work to let workers decide if they need protecting."*

So the Labor Department sued CB Sports, Inc. Arthur O'Dea, attorney in Manchester, representing CB Sports, Inc., was very pessimistic of the chances for defeating the government, which was defeating the life plan and initiative of these Vermonters.

Fortunately, the people in this Vermont community were able to mobilize public sentiment and bring the issue to the attention of the Congress. Several of the women traveled to Washington at their own expense to tell the national legislators what they thought of this effort to protect them from themselves. The Labor Department fought them all the way, but this time common sense prevailed. Congress passed an exemption to the 1938 law allowing the industrious Vermonters to continue their gainful independence.

Encouraging? Sort of. Until you stop to think of the monumental effort necessary to win government acceptance of the kind of independent initiative that built this country into a prosperous free society. And for every hard-won victory, a score of bureaucratic efforts are put into motion to ensure that citizens live and work by the book of federal regulation, whether that proves in their interests or not.

Government routinely defeats initiative that it does not have the perception to identify.

Worse still, it does not have the perception to see that cottage industry on a national scale could become a huge modern breakthrough in solving gigantic problems of unemployment, productivity, and inflation.

For example, Donna Puccini of Arlington Heights, Illinois, resigned as a legal secretary to have a baby. Later, though thrilled with her baby girl, Angelina, Donna became bored with housework. Making an arrangement with Continental Illinois Bank, Donna now has in her bedroom a computerized word processor on which she types letters for the company. They are flashed to the office over telephone wires. In a *Wall Street Journal* article by Ray Vicker, she stated, "This is perfect for me, working at home, with my baby playing on the floor."

Human ingenuity made the special telecommunications equipment that made it possible for Donna to earn a paycheck and still tend her baby. The paycheck incentive and Donna's initiative made her a happy woman and a taxpayer.

The *Wall Street Journal* article estimates that 50,000 people are in a situation to take advantage of working at home with computer assistance.

That would have tremendous positive impact upon the nation's productivity and income. But our government is not in favor of cottage industries.

In Chicago, thirty-four-year-old Carlos Rodriquez bought from the United States Housing and Urban Development Department (HUD) a house on West 106th Street to remodel and resell.

A good carpenter, Rodriquez put on a new roof, two new

porches, gutters, downspouts, aluminum siding, and paint. He worked rapidly because he wanted to sell it quickly, get back his capital and buy another for remodeling.

He installed a new furnace, water heater, some new wiring, new bath and kitchen fixtures. He paneled the kitchen, recarpeted six rooms, and one staircase.

To move it quickly, he priced the house moderately at $28,000, which quickly drew a lady buyer. All she wanted changed was the color of paint in one bedroom. Rodriquez went out, bought the paint, and drove out to his house on West 106th Street.

It was gone.

Neighbors told him a wrecking crew demolished it two days ago.

City Hall explained. They had a year-old order to demolish, with a written order from HUD, then owner. Nobody had bothered to check to see that Rodriquez was the new owner.

HUD and the city of Chicago bounced Rodriquez back and forth. Neither would pay him for the bureaucratic boner.

To collect, he would have to sue the United States government. His lawyer, Ted Musberger, told him that would require at least three years.

Meanwhile Carlos has no capital to continue. His government defeated his initiative and his life plan.

Multiply that incident by thousands.

Is it common sense for our own government to put us out of business?

In Wichita, Kansas, Richard Saunders operated a small sixty-man foundry, casting components for the wing flaps for 747s and control gates for Lear Jets.

Saunders is a lean, leathery engineer in his sixties whom some aircraft people consider a near genius, but he is the old school, straight-on type, very inept at compromise. He tells suppliers, "Name your best price first, because I won't come back to haggle."

His foundry was considered by some the nation's most modern and efficient. A Boeing executive called it "undoubtedly the cleanest damned foundry I've ever been in."

Two OSHA inspectors (Occupational Safety and Health Administration) walked in to inspect. Previous OSHA inspectors had given the plant high praise. This time Mr. Saunders came down through the plant to find one of the new OSHA men instructing a group of his employees how they could get hurt on the job. Saunders exclaimed, "That's the stupidest damn thing I ever heard."

Soon after that remark, four OSHA inspectors arrived. In a retaliatory mood, they wrote up twenty-three alleged "serious safety law violations."

When this happens, it is customary for the company to sit down and bargain, accepting some violations and OSHA giving up some. But Saunders is not a negotiating type. A new explosion-proof dust collector that OSHA required would cost $500,000. Saunders considered this damn foolery because he had his grinders operating in booths with suction equipment drawing off metal dust.

Although the company had orders booked halfway through the ensuing year, Saunders felt that borrowing a half million for unnecessary safety devices would be a step toward bankruptcy, considering annual sales were only $8 million. He put the question to his informal board of directors. They agreed.

On May 30, 1980, the machinery was auctioned off. Saunders' government defeated the life plan of his sixty employees and himself.

Jeff Spahn, OSHA director for Kansas, according to *The Wall Street Journal*, was surprised that the foundry closed. "I can show you case after case where we negotiated procedures...that were less strict. There are many ways to skin a cat."

Over three hundred foundries in the United States have closed because of OSHA regulations. Our government has put thousands out of work and defeated a vital U.S. industry more effectively than an enemy attack.

To fill the gap left by our closed foundries, "India is flooding this country," according to foundry owner Jim Pinkerton of Lodi, California. "We spent $500,000 in the last year for nonproductive equipment to satisfy various regulations. That's why we can't compete with foreign foundries."

Meanwhile military castings are being imported at high cost. This is common sense?

In Painesville, Ohio, the county commissioners were eager to have the new county administration building finished because it was to spark a general urban renewal. But completion was held up because they couldn't get the Bangor roof slate specified by the architect.

Irritated by the delay, one commissioner phoned Charles E. Smith, president of North Bangor Slate Company in Bangor, Pennsylvania. Smith told him to blame excessive federal regulation for the problem: "I was for many years the largest producer of roofing slate in the United States. But that was before I was bedeviled by the Bureau of Mines and the EPA.

"I spent about $20,000 to meet their regulations. At my peak I had two hundred men working three quarries. Now there are only between seven and ten people in the whole state of Pennsylvania making slate.

"Who would want to start a quarry when you have fifty government men standing over you? You are better off becoming a bank teller."

Foreign nations laugh as we hog-tie our own strengths and wreck our industries so that imports can take over our market. Our once-great auto industry is crippled as our Highway Traffic Safety Administration orders heavy safety features for cars even as the Transportation Department orders lighter vehicles to save fuel. EPA restricts pesticide use while the Department of Agriculture promotes it. Part of government restricts resource development on its lands, while another part demands increased energy production. The EPA pushes for tough air pollution control while the Department of Energy pushes industry to switch from imported oil to sulfurous coal.

Twelve different agencies and thirty-one sizeable subdivisions of the federal government have an impact on coal use, production, and transportation. To open a new mine, coal operators need permits from between fifteen and twenty different regulatory agencies. Government presence postpones action.

Energy is a major national need, of course. Corwin D. Denny, in a major address at Pepperdine University entitled, *The Free World's Energy Crisis,* documented in detail his opening thesis: "government intervention decades ago, into the U.S. oil and gas industry, resulting in almost complete removal of the free enterprise environment, has directly caused the mess we are in."

A major national need for the 1980s is housing. A formidable roadblock is our own government. Adding as much as 25 percent to the cost of a house is a maze of government regulations and codes discouraging the use of the most modern and efficient construction methods. Again, our government is our enemy.

The Council on Wage and Price Stability has revealed the steel industry to be subject to 5,600 separate federal regulations from twenty-nine agencies administering fifty-seven programs. Obviously, if the government decides to harass or persecute an industry, "there is more than one way to skin a cat." There are so many ways, in fact, that there is no possibility of avoiding the ridiculous.

For example, OSHA has mandated backup alarms on vehicles on a construction site while simultaneously ordering workmen to wear earplugs.

That would be a laugh if it wasn't destroying us.

How Did This Happen?

We did it.

We allowed a new branch of government to create itself, unelected by the people, unprovided for in the Constitution, uncontrollable by Congress, unanswerable to the executive branch, and overwhelming to the courts.

It stands—powerful, massive, overpowering the constitutional branches of government—its objectives antithetical to the people.

This is common sense?

This federal regulatory group takes a small congressional bill and re-interprets it into hundreds of federal regulations. . .adopting powers far beyond anything Congress envisioned.

Certainly some protection is needed, but the protector has become the threat.

The Unelected Government of the United States

All the foregoing havoc is from only a *few* damaging federal agencies throwing the nation to the mat.

Now comes the shocker. There is an 843-page book[1] more than three inches thick, weighing nearly three pounds, listing

1. *The Federal Regulatory Directory* 1983-84, published by Congressional Quarterly, Inc. (not part of the government) to help us find our way through our monstrous regulatory federal government.

and briefly defining hundreds more such destructive federal bodies which regulate our lives and destroy precious initiative. This book does *not* include township, city, county, or state regulatory bodies.

The 1970s saw gargantuan regulatory growth. The Federal Register, official record of new and revised federal regulations, grew from 20,036 pages in 1970 to 61,000 in 1978. Even with the Reagan administration's much-vaunted effort to reduce regulations, the 1983 Federal Register numbered 57,704 pages.

Thousands of men and women we never elected now form a fourth branch of government we never authorized, setting policy and creating regulations governing us. And these people are generally unknown.

President Carter, in a message to Congress on March 26, 1979, said, "The overall system has become burdensome. No one has analyzed the benefits or costs, and in spite of changing conditions, many regulatory programs have been allowed to continue unreviewed for decades."

I draw my idea of the form of government from a principle in nature which no art can overturn, viz., that the more simple anything is, the less liable it is to be disordered and the easier repaired when disordered.
—Common Sense

Agreeing with Carter, Congress originated more than 150 bills addressing the problem, but there was no relief. Even today, approximately 100,000 federal regulators are at work for the forty-eight most powerful agencies. They work through some 1,200 boards, commissions, and committees, at stupefying costs.

While the legal authority for federal regulation is contained in the commerce clause of the Constitution, Article I, Section 8, the economic rationale for regulation is not so clear. By the 1970s, the rationality and the expertise of regulatory agencies were being widely questioned.

Since regulation is as old as man, what is the objection to modern U.S. regulations? Unbridled, unsupervised power.

During the nineteenth century, government regulation was almost entirely by statutes and enforced through the courts. That was fine. The distinguishing feature of current twentieth-century governmental regulation is that the legislatures provide only a broad mandate, leaving an agency enormous discretion to implement it. *The agency has the power to prescribe regulations that have the force of law, to police those subject to its authority, and to decide cases involving possible violations—the legislative, executive, and judicial powers all rolled into one body.*

That is raw power.

Men who look upon themselves both to reign and others to obey soon grow insolent. Selected from the rest of mankind, their minds are early poisoned by importance.

—Common Sense

Even President Roosevelt's committee to study the regulatory process described the commissions as "...a headless fourth branch of the government, a haphazard deposit of irresponsible agencies and uncoordinated powers. They do violence to the basic theory of the American Constitution that there should be three major branches of the government and only three. The Congress has found no effective way of supervising them, they cannot be controlled by the president, and they are answerable to the courts only in respect to the legality of their activities."

Five recent presidents have tried to leash these bureaus, which really have no boss.

No one has succeeded.

How do regulatory bodies defeat America? In several ways; one is by delays.

The ICC had one merger case pending six years, and the FTC had a case in the works for more than thirteen years. The FCC has taken as long as five years to decide between competing applicants for a television channel.

The Federal Power Commission once estimated "that it would take thirteen years with its (then) present staff to clear up its pending 2,313 producer rate cases pending as of July 1, 1960, and that with the contemplated 6,500 cases which would be filed during that thirteen-year period, it could not become current until 2043 A.D., even if its staff were tripled."

The regulatory agencies have put the nation on hold.

Delay destroys development, discouraging investment. Pharmaceutical houses are notably gun-shy of investing in new product development because FDA regulations are so inordinately cumbersome when it comes to approving new drugs.

Statistics compiled by the U.S. Administrative Conference and the Senate Committee on Government Operations reveal the following: On average it takes an agency
- more than nineteen months to issue a license;
- twenty-one months to get through rate-making proceedings;
- over three years for enforcement actions;
- in licensing and rate-making, 160 days for cases *even to reach* the hearing state.

It takes the ICC 915 days to complete proceedings on approval of rail abandonment, mergers, or securities issues by rail or water carriers or freight forwarders.

The regulators are defeating America without a shot being fired.

Kamikaze Costs

Any military opponent of the United States will be thrilled by the impoverishing regulatory invoice we pay. The tremendous cost of these whimsical regulations is frightening. Senator Thomas F. Eagleton (D-Mo.) in 1979 pointed out, "Regulations cost American business an estimated $102 billion a year, about $30 billion of it in mountains of paperwork. All this adds to the crushing burden of inflation."

A Dow Chemical Company study showed the impact of federal regulations recently cost the company $185 million, a 27 percent increase over two years before.

The University of Pennsylvania found that to comply with twelve federally regulated programs, costs jumped in five years from $350,000 per year to $3.2 million.

The object contended for ought always to bear some just proportion to the expense.

—Common Sense

These costs are not somebody else's money. It's yours. To cite one everyday instance, federal regulation of milk prices in one recent year cost consumers about 10 percent of their milk bills, nearly $1 billion.

The pharmaceutical firm of Eli Lilly & Co. estimates the cost of an average prescription goes up fifty cents each year to pay the expense of new federal regulations.

The American Hospital Association estimated that in complying with just eight regulations, its member institutions spent $800 million in 1976, adding $22 to the average hospital bill. The cost today is substantially higher.

Economist Murray Weidenbaum has estimated that the average family of four in the United States pays an extra $2,000 a year as a result of regulations. "Virtually every study of regulatory experience indicates both needless expense and ineffective operations."

And by a plain method of argument, as we are running the next generation into debt, we ought to do the work of it; otherwise we use them meanly and pitifully.

—Common Sense

A couple of years ago *Purchasing Magazine* estimated that the cost of government regulation ran as high as $134.8 billion per year. Included in that was $2 billion for productivity lost by employees just spending time dealing with regulations.

But there's an additional hidden cost of government regulation, according to Weidenbaum—its adverse effect on innovation. "The longer it takes for a new product to be approved by a government agency—or the more costly the approval process— the less likely that the new product will be created."

The bureaus are defeating America...and sending us the bill on top of it all.

Priority Targets

While an enemy of the United States would not target in on Joe Pinga's bakery nor Susan Walsh's ski cap business, they *would* consider it a perfect strike to knock out the entire U.S. foundry industry. What else would they consider prime target accomplishments? These:

- Destroy the basic democratic procedures, which can unleash tremendous power;

- Destroy small business, which furnishes the buoyancy of competition and over half the nation's jobs;
- Destroy big industry, with its tremendous development capability;
- Destroy employment;
- Destroy the American energy supply.

If an enemy general staff could accomplish all this, they would have us licked and would consider the attack worth a tremendous cost to their nation. However, it might not cost them a dime.

We are seeing the destruction of the nation's basic democratic procedures. U.S. regulatory agencies bypass democratic procedures and employ raw power they were never explicitly granted. For example, the EPA wants to require twenty-nine states to set up special auto emissions inspection stations in certain areas. In these stations, motorists would be charged $20 for emissions inspections.

The California legislature refused.

To coerce California, the EPA set out to have $700 million in federal highway and sewer funds withheld. EPA also threatened to delay industrial expansion by delaying approval of California industry environmental impact statements. That is raw power.

The California legislature fought this power play, but Colorado knuckled under to an EPA threat to withhold $300 million.

Colorado Senate President Fred Anderson pointed out that no one gave EPA the right to perform the function of state legislators, but they were in effect doing it anyway, destroying democratic processes.

We are seeing the destruction of small business. Joe Pinga fought them off his bakery, but we have seen the regulators effectively shut down our whole foundry industry, made up of small companies manufacturing the basic castings for engines, machine tools, and vehicles. Castings are the backbones of industrial America.

This is common sense?

Few know that small business (companies employing five hundred or less people) employs just over half the working people in the nation. Therefore, when we destroy small businesses we are destroying a very important national economic resource.

The Small Business Administration is little help. Business associations consider the SBA a dumping ground for political hacks with no business experience. The services offered are abstract, obscure, and trivial. SBA should be disbanded.

We are seeing the destruction of big industry development. The dismantling of the greatest production economy in the world by regulatory action amazes our enemies even as they applaud. They can't believe their eyes.

U.S. Steel proposed a huge new plant in Conneaut, Ohio. It required two years for a permit granting approval. At the then inflation rate, that raised the cost $100,000 per day. The plant would have employed 8,000 people. Thirty miles across Lake Erie from Conneaut, a Canadian steel company that started at the same time completed its plant and was in production two years later. U.S. Steel has still not broken ground at Conneaut. The project is probably no longer under consideration.

Deere & Co. in Dubuque, Iowa, used to get a dredging permit in three weeks. It now takes three years. Dow Chemical abandoned building a half-billion-dollar complex in San Francisco when 2 1/2 years and $4 million got it only four of the sixty-five required permits.

At a time when the government is urging energy suppliers to find new production, the EPA was only just stopped from making a regulation that an oil company be required to file a 300-day advance notice of intent to drill a well and to get a permit to use drilling mud.

Under EPA regs, it now takes about seven years and $7 million, according to the American Association of Poison Control Centers, to bring out a new pesticide.

To bring out a new drug is nearly unthinkable. Eli Wood, chairman of Eli Lilly, says that his company spends more on government forms than on researching heart and cancer disease. One application to FDA to bring out a new arthritis drug totaled 120,000 pages.

The fourth branch of government is recklessly converting us to a backward nation.

We are seeing the destruction of employment. We have seen government create massive, immediate unemployment in key industries like steel and autos. Nearly as serious is the *future* unemployment of teenagers now trying to get a foot on the vocational ladders. Making it illegal to hire them for less than minimum wage does not raise their standard of living. It simply means they don't get jobs. They wind up with a zero standard of living.

There have been efforts to make changes. Companies or persons with fewer than ten employees have greater leeway with respect to minimum wage requirements. And a concerted drive is under way to exempt teens, among whom unemployment is at astronomical levels. But even so, short-sighted paternalists in government continue to insist on the need to include teens and job-hungry unskilled laborers under the illusory umbrella of minimum wage protection.

We are seeing the destruction of freedom to work at home. Government has taken aim at people working at home, using the sweatshop laws. Homework is seldom sweatshop work today. Even when it is, since it is voluntary, everyone should have the right to sweat if he wants.

With the destruction of democratic process, the destruction of small business, the destruction of big industry development, and the destruction of employment, would a foreign enemy need to fire a single shot to see us reduced to a noncompetitive, second-rate power?

The government exacerbates the energy problem. The illusion of cheap energy fostered by government price controls encouraged production of large, gas-glutton cars. This shielded Americans from the true world petroleum supply-and-demand picture. Given wrong economic signals, industry responded with the wrong products.

Had the government not created the illusion of "cheap energy," the automotive industry might have converted to the fuel-efficient car in time to save itself the enormous losses racked up in the first years of this decade.

The solution that became the problem. The Department of Energy, a monster 20,000 bureaucrats strong, with a $12.5 billion budget (more than the cost of our oil imports from Saudi Arabia!) was organized to solve the energy shortage. Its budget quickly exceeded the earnings of the eight largest oil companies, while its efforts largely impeded their search for new sources of energy.

Senator Thomas F. Eagleton (D-Mo.), one of the original

supporters of the DOE, not long after described its record as "an unbroken string of bellyflops."

Some of the bellyflops are evident in these news notes:

Sohio abandons Pactex. Informs shareholders that the once-attractive economics of the proposed Pacific Coast to Texas pipeline is being abandoned because of "seemingly endless government red tape in obtaining key permits."

Stripper oil wells quit. Oil wells that produce less than ten barrels a day are being forced out of business because of the windfall profits tax. Closing such wells, predicted the Interstate Oil Company Commission, representing thirty oil-producing states, will lose us 175 million annual barrels of oil.

Mobil builds its coal conversion plant, not in USA but in New Zealand. "That country made a national decision it wants to do this," said Joe E. Penick, president of Mobil Research & Development Corporation.

General Accounting Office (GAO) and the Office of Technology Assessment (OTA) claim half the government's solar projects are inoperable.

Imagine the confusion and frustration of those trying to work with the department during the following rather typical changes. The DOE was the FPC (Federal Power Commission) connected to the ERA (Economic Regulatory Administration) governed by the FERC (Federal Energy Regulatory Commission), formerly the FEA (Federal Energy Administration) and connected to the ERDA (Energy Research and Development Administration) which was connected to the FEO (Federal Energy Office) but replaced by the FEA, which became ERA. Got that? (And if we got it wrong, it's not because we missed an easy turn somewhere.) Old energy bureaus never die, they just get renamed.

Our enemies love us. We defeat ourselves.

Why Can't Congress Control the Monsters It Created?

Oklahoma Senator David L. Boren, formerly a state legislator and governor, went to Washington expecting to make some changes. "What impressed me most is the great power of the bureaucracy compared to that of elected officials. All the talk about growing control by the bureaucracy is not exaggerated. *The shift in power is very real."*

Boren found that over the years Congress has delegated away so much power that 80 percent of the laws are made by bureaucrats not accountable to the people. "There is almost a contempt for elected officials."

Men who look upon themselves born to reign and others to obey soon grow insolent.

—Common Sense

Senator Boren found, to his surprise, that a senator has great difficulty even getting phone calls returned by the "permanent" employees much less getting responsive answers to his questions.

The voters can't "throw the rascals out" anymore, because the main rascals are not elected but appointed.

Boren especially feels our national productivity problem is the inevitable product of overregulation by government, making it "almost impossible for private companies to make long-range investment decisions." Boren says the regulatory agencies can create exactly the opposite effect of Congressional intent.

For example, Congress wanted more accountability for payment of hospital medical services. "We urged HEW (now the Health and Human Services Department) to set up a review process to make sure medical services were being provided in a cost effective way. Well, they came up with a rule that for every major service performed, you had to have three other doctors write a report on how effective that treatment was, whether it was the cheapest method, and so on.

However, in rural states half the hospitals have three or fewer doctors. Since such hospitals could not come up with three other doctors, "they were going to close 40 percent of the hospitals in Oklahoma. We were going to be sending people two hundred to three hundred miles to get to a hospital."

That is typical, Boren warns, of how a regulation "completely undid the whole purpose of the legislation."

To give some idea of the mass of this damage, on one given day in November of 1981, three thousand proposed rules were moving through the pipeline. Squelching this proliferation of garbage is imperative.

Regulatory bureaucrats have extra power because they can outlast the elected officials. "Often," Boren explains, "I've said to a bureaucrat, 'You know this is not the President's policy.' "

"True, Senator. but we were here before he came, and we'll be here after he leaves. We're not in sympathy with his policy. We'll study the matter until he leaves."

A lot of power accrues to regulators and bureaus because they are great largely unaccountable dispensers of money to their own large nonelectoral constituencies.

Since our legislators can't control the regulators, the citizen must.

How?

The First Step

Most regulatory functions can be handled better by ourselves.

Start very close to home—consumer protection. We can do that better than government.

Thomas A. Murphy, former chairman of General Motors, once observed, "In most cases the consumer shopping for maximum value is a far more stern disciplinarian than any commissioner in Washington. And he can carry out this regulatory function immediately and at zero cost in new taxation."

If that is not enough protection, we can organize private organizations to do a better job than government. The idea behind the highly effective Good Housekeeping Seal of Approval can be replicated in all product categories. So can the idea behind the UL (Underwriters Laboratories) seal on your electrical appliances. This is a private form of buyer protection. No government coercion is involved, yet to market an electrical product without that UL watchdog seal of approval today would be very difficult.

The standards committees of the various trade associations also publish standards of quality to be met. Not to meet these standards in manufacturing grinding wheels or fireproof doors or I-beams is a form of industrial suicide.

But of course the best mechanism of all is good hard-nosed comparative shopping.

Energy. Unhampered by U.S. government, Cities Service and four joint venture partners opened up the huge Syncrude plant in Athabasca region of Alberta, Canada, extracting oil from the tar sands. It wasn't long before the Syncrude plant was producing 125,000 barrels a day.

Industry can solve energy problems.

Not long ago the government launched a grant-loan program to develop methane from garbage. *But this was already being done* on a private commercial basis by nine large plants. The companies already working landfills to produce methane had invested in the necessary research and development. When government offered landfill money to reinvent a process, it caused the landfills to balk at making their garbage available to private processors in hopes of getting government research money for themselves.

Pollution. We have created the enormous, well-intended EPA organization and given it an assignment it cannot possibly do—clean up the environment.

The common-sense solution is probably contained in these three steps:

1. Legislate to establish long-range environmental standards.
2. Prompt the industries and organizations involved (which include government polluters) to assume responsibility for achieving these standards.
3. Encourage these industries, as necessary, to enlist the research help of universities, which could receive charitable support by the 20/20 charity support plan described in Chapter 3. This should reduce drastically the tax load on the citizens.

Can industry handle its own pollution?

The evidence is that it can.

The chemicals industry, considered one of the largest polluters, is doing possibly the biggest cleanup. The motivation is not altruistic. The industry is trying to cut waste and increase productivity. To do this, the chemical producers are investing more than any other industry—25 cents out of every dollar the industry spends on new manufacturing facilities goes for pollution control. The industry has put more than 10,000 employees to work full-time on pollution control, fighting pollution a number of ways—aeration, biological treatment, flotation, separation...using any cleanup technology that works.

They reuse pollutants. For example, wastes containing nitrogen from one chemical plant are now processed to provide nutrition for pine trees; sulfuric acid waste waters are being contained and neutralized to produce gypsum for wallboard and cement.

This is the way to go, strengthening ourselves instead of defeating ourselves.

How to Get the Bureaus Off the Taxpayer's Back

Every government service worth keeping, except for the military, can be self-financing.

The FDIC is funded by assessments levied against member banks. The Federal Reserve System is also funded by its member banks.

The Interior Department could be funded in the same way. Interior includes the Bureau of Indian Affairs, the Office of Land Management, the U.S. Fish & Wildlife Service, and Geological Survey. With no changes in functions, this department could be financed by license fees, direct taxation to recipients of services, and the sale of natural resources and land.

The Justice Department includes Antitrust, Civil Rights, the Drug Enforcement Administration, Immigration and Naturalization Service, and Law Enforcement Assistance. The department could merge divisions with similar functions. It could use antitrust law enforcement only as last resort after all normal competitive business possibilities are encouraged, including free foreign trade. A reduced budget allocation in proportion to scaled-down activities would reduce the load on the taxpayers.

The Labor Department includes Employment Standards Administration, Employment & Training, Labor-Management Relations, and Mine Safety & Health Administration. We suggest eliminating functions that cannot be supported by direct billing of those receiving the services; a transfer of retirement fiduciary standards and similar functions to the IRS; a transfer of statistical work to private labor associations.

The Transportation Department includes the administrations of Federal Aviation, Federal Highway, Federal Railroad, Materials Transportation, National Highway Traffic Safety, St. Lawrence Seaway Development Corporation, U.S. Coast Guard and Urban Mass Transportation Administration. Again, we suggest eliminating all functions that cannot be supported by direct invoicing of those receiving services. This would work. These costs would be passed on, but correctly, to the user. Only the Coast Guard should be retained as taxpayer-supported and possibly transferred to the Defense Department.

In all areas, we feel price and production controls are best handled by competition.

The Treasury Department includes Bureau of Alcohol, Tobacco and Firearms, Comptroller of the Currency, Internal Revenue Service, Office of Tariff Affairs, and U.S. Customs Service. We suggest retaining all nonduplicating functions and financing as many of these as possible by direct taxation on users or by tariffs.

Nearly every necessary agency could be handled in this manner, including those with a research function. Some part of the civilian research establishment has reason to attack nearly every problem. For example, University of Miami biochemist Dr. Daniel G. Baden recently isolated a crucial ingredient in the red tide that has attacked the Florida coasts from time to time. He found it contains two toxins, both potent killers of marine life. This discovery is a major step toward a solution. The Florida hospitality industry and/or the Florida fisheries industry can logically fund further research. This is an example of transferring work to nongovernment hands.

Standing in the way, of course, are the entrenched staffs of bureaus prepared to fight reduction of personnel.

What the Coming Generation Must Do About It

Why the coming generation?

Because the generation now in control will never get the job done. We allowed this crisis to develop right in front of our eyes, step by step. We never added up the accumulating disaster. Additionally, the older generation will not live long enough.

To repair the damage, a two-phase campaign must be launched.

Phase one: Get the regulatory agencies under control. Then control the controls. That can be done. Practical methods for this are now gaining strength.

Phase two: Eliminate some regulatory agencies and transfer the useful parts of their function to the private sector.

"E-lim-i-nate? Totally eliminate?"

Yes. Don't be alarmed. There is no need to destroy any essential service the agencies provide.

Why do this thing in two steps, instead of one? Only because elimination of some agencies will require considerable time. Meanwhile, they must be brought under the control of the elected representatives, and ultimately under the control of the citizens to whom they now have zero accountability.

Implementing Phase One

Phase one has several steps. While working to control all the agencies, you also need to control the yet unborn agencies. Therefore *push very hard to pass all the sunset laws.*

This is achievable. Some sunset laws are already in place. Sunset laws set a time after which the agency must go out of business. If needed, the agency can be reborn with a new enabling act. The momentum favoring sunset laws is already rolling. Push it.

Next...*set overall regulatory goals instead of specific methods of achieving those goals.* Let industry figure out how to meet the goals. The government is not the best-equipped body for making a car or a vaccine safe.

Repeal all excessive and outdated regulations now.

Require regulations invented by the agencies to be subject to review and veto by legislatures on a specific timetable. This is already beginning.

Deregulate where possible with the same gusto that bred regulation. This is already beginning. Push it.

Eliminate overlapping and conflicting regulations.

Implementing Phase Two

The prospect of eliminating will certainly arouse a horrendous howl. Over the years, the agencies have each developed powerful constituencies that they can call up to their defense in emergencies. The Department of Agriculture, for example, can mobilize regiments of farmers as troops to defend itself.

But start with common sense. Such agency functions as the people *need and want* can, of course, be preserved. Which risks are to be ignored and which reduced? Mr. Lave, professor at Carnegie Mellon University, says in *The Wall Street Journal*, "Two principles would be of enormous help: (1) Ignore minimal risks, and (2) balance risks against benefits and control costs where risks are not negligible." Any functions that can *best* be delivered by a government regulatory agency can certainly be continued. But *all functions that can be delivered best by nongovernmental agencies should be.* That includes most of them.

We do not need babysitters. Individual citizens deciding what work they will do under what conditions for how much money is how we will get the big work of this country done.

Coke ovens are the hottest, dirtiest work places in steel-making. But the pay is great. Jasper H. Hoven worked the coke oven at Republic Steel in Cleveland for fifteen years. He had a good record. The company decided he had earned a job in a less challenging environment. They gave him a choice of three cleaner jobs. He refused. There was more overtime available on the coke ovens. He liked the money. He could take the heat.

It's his decision.

It's common sense.

The Proper Attitude of the Citizen Toward Regulatory Agencies

While it might seem extreme, the proper attitude of a United States citizen is that displayed by Violet Smith, Hay Gulch, Colorado. Hay Gulch is a very small town, but important because the American independent spirit still thrives there. It's where Violet Smith lives.

Violet and her husband operate a small coal mine next to their home and have done so without assistance or advice from the government since 1936. Violet is in her seventies; her work-lined face is serene and reflects her whole history.

When federal coal mine inspectors back in the mid-seventies came to tell her that she was going to have to build a bathhouse next to the mine, she chased them off her property. "My house is next to the mine," she commented tersely. "What in hell do I need with a bathhouse?"

An Associated Press story about Violet explained that she has no regard for mine inspectors, and has "run 'em off with a pick handle once, and a two-by-four...oh yeah, I chased one little s.o.b. with a butcher knife. But I never drew my gun."

Her most affectionate reference to mine inspectors is "them pissants" and her dispute with them started when they tried to enforce mine safety rules that Violet feels were written by jackasses and anyhow couldn't apply to her modest coal mine.

The same year the inspectors had their bathhouse run-in with Violet was the year the state presented her an award for safety at the mine.

Violet has a sign on her property: "No inspectors allowed. This is our property. We are capable of minding our own business."

Now *that* is the correct attitude.

ULTRA SECRET

TO: General Officers Only

Addendum to Earlier Memo

In conquering the United States, one of our greatest obstacles will be the nation's spirit of individual independence and creative initiative. We have been counting upon the ever expanding and intrusive American bureaucracy to snuff out this spirit, as per previous memorandum.

However, there is evidence that bureaucratic excesses are alerting parts of the U.S. civil population to its own danger from within. This awakening would undermine our campaign for the bloodless defeat of America.

All espionage units will double propaganda efforts to keep America asleep.

By Order,
Commander-in-Chief
All Forces Opposing the USA

5

MORE FOR
YOUR MONEY

The Best of Enemies

Do you have a U.S. quarter handy?

Run your fingernail around the edge. This is important.

Feel those serrations? That is called the *milling*. It is not deco-
ration, it was not initiated by the government coin designer.

Those rim ridges were demanded by the citizenry to detect
and head off tyranny imposed by our hired government via inflation. In the days when coins were actually made of precious
metals, milling guarded against government "shaving" coins to
make them less valuable.

We will waste no time defining inflation.

But just to refresh you on the hazard, if you are thirty years
old, and if inflation continues at only five percent a year, what
will you pay for bread upon your retirement at age sixty-five?
The answer: around $5.25. That would put a $10,000 car at
$50,000. Yet that is not as severe as the shrinkage we've suf-
fered in the last thirty-five years, during which a loaf of bread
went from costing a dime to a dollar.

True, pay scales will rise more or less proportionately, so what's the difference? The difference is that it wipes out the buying power of your previous savings; and if you are retired on a fixed income from those savings, it changes you from an honored retiree to someone living in poverty. By the time you are sixty-five, the baby boom wave will be retiring, so we are talking about huge numbers of people, all cheated by inflation. But tyranny via *inflation?* How could that be? *That is* an invisible progression we don't understand, but via inflation we're burrowing like blind moles right back into what Tom Paine called a "state of vassalage."

Inflation leads directly to tyranny. It is what gave birth to Franco, Mussolini, and Hitler. As people impoverished by inflation finally have to struggle for necessities, anarchy breaks out. First people beg government to step in and allocate, say, the potatoes. . . then all resources. That naturally requires total control by government force. But government first *creates* that inflation, and not by accident. It is so hard to believe they would do that to us that we need to feel the edge of that quarter, the reminder that the most patriotic attitude of a citizen toward the government he loves is to keep a sharp eye on it.

. . . but government in its best state is but a necessary evil; in its worst state an intolerable one; for when we suffer, or are exposed to the same miseries by a government, which we might expect without government, our calamity is heightened by reflecting that we furnish the means by which we suffer.
—Common Sense

We did not keep an eye on our government in 1934. That year the government banged the gold door shut to Americans. That in turn opened the door to inflation and big government and loss of liberty.

Since there are no milled edges that we can feel on a dollar bill, we cannot feel clearly what the government was doing to our money. By prohibiting citizens from dealing in gold (which always sets a standard of value recognizable to everyone in the open marketplace), the government in 1934 was shaving our currency.

Shaving?

In frontier times, people understood shaving. On a day before milled-edge coins in the United States, John Wiler, owner of a frontier tavern in Wooster, Ohio, entered the store of G. V. Robinson & E. O. Jones, Drygoods, Queenswear & Groceries. He picked out thirty large tins of tea. Then, under the scrutiny of Robinson, he placed two silver dollars in two shallow circular indentations augured into the counter top.

Wiler usually held back his silver and paid in paper. The Ohio frontier was laced with forty-three kinds of official and wildcat paper currency that dropped in buying power about a penny a mile as it traveled away from its issuing bank. You tried to get rid of your paper money quick and close to home.

A hand-lettered chart on Robinson & Jones' store wall listed the dozen paper currencies acceptable in this store and at what discounts. The bottom notation read, "Silver dollars accepted at 50 percent bonus." But the offerer had to place his dollar in the round augur hole in the counter top. Robinson had to see if Wiler's coins fit snug in the template. Or had they been shaved?

Hans F. Sennholz, chairman of the Economics Department of Grove City College and a longtime analyst of world inflation, graphically explains shaving in his *Age of Inflation*. Governments throughout history engineered inflation deliberately, as a method of taxing their own people. "Thus," Sennholz points out, "a government debt [i.e., your war bonds] of $40 billion 1940 dollars can now be paid off...with a 1978 dollar issue worth less than 20 percent of the original amount.... Millions of patriotic citizen creditors thus now can be swindled out of their rightful claims and their property quietly confiscated." And this is by the government hired to make them "secure in their property."

But Sennholz's real warning cry is not that inflation impoverishes people, but that "*Few policies are more calculated to destroy...a free society than the debauching of its currency.*"

Whenever governments have had to raise huge revenues for wars, road building, or other sweeping projects for which their people would refuse new visible taxation, they have instructed their agents to shave the coinage. Using hard knives, agents trimmed a little silver or gold off the circumference of the coinage on its normal flow through the treasury or government banks.

Cheating each citizen of tiny slivers generally escaped broad notice or complaint, and among the knowledgeable it inspired only cynical winks—"The government is shaving again." But this pile of shavings added up to large additional revenues for governments.

When merchants became aware of it, they merely raised their prices to offset the shaving. Inflation.

When the coins would stand no further shaving, they were recalled; new ones were issued in smaller size, but with the same denomination embossed on the face. Inflation, institutionalized.

Sometimes citizens shaved the coins. Same result. Inflation.

Robinson put his finger on Wiler's silver dollar and tried to wiggle it in the slot to see if it had been shaved. It was a snug fit, so Wiler walked out with this tea.

However, in normal workaday trade in the street markets, sellers could hardly have an augured hole always handy to inspect for shaved money.

To make detection easier, the people demanded milling around the edges of coins. You couldn't shave the coin without destroying the milling.

However, there is no such milling to detect the shaving of paper dollars. Someone has yet to invent a milling for paper dollars. The best milling may be citizens constantly checking the dollar against the price of gold. Meet us in Chapter 8 for the citizen action required.

Paper dollars are shaved simply by issuing *more* of them. That just as surely waters down the value of currency. Inflation.

It is a vastly surer, swifter, and more appealing way for governments to raise money than trying to legislate a visible tax. Shaving, however, is exactly that, a tax deliberately assessed and collected, but invisible, thus bypassing "the consent of the governed." To pay its bills, our government sells treasury bills, notes, and bonds, and creates money. So doing it secretly drinks half from our flask of wine, then fills it up with water so we won't notice. Taxation by inflation.

"Inflation is a tax? Isn't the government equally a *victim* of inflation?"

No. It is a beneficiary. A sales tax on a $6,000 Oldsmobile gives the government less tax revenue than the sales tax on that same car when the price inflates to $15,000. Inflation is hidden "taxation without representation," the cause of our celebrated

Boston Tea Party. It is time for a Washington Tea Party.

Inflation leads us to tyranny in two steps. Step One, after watering down the currency, government fiat finally is required to make merchants *accept* the watered-down money for food and other necessities. This historically fails; goods won't move. So then Step Two, government force must allocate the food supply. Then shelter. Then everything.

In frontier times, when paper dollars went bad we switched to bucks. When a buck was a buck, meaning the skin of a full-grown buck deer, we were free of inflation and tyranny. The value was right in the buckskin. If you didn't want to spend it, you could wear it. You could spend it with strangers, because you didn't have to explain it or justify it. The value was obviously in the money itself.

Unfortunately, buckskins were unhandy to carry in quantity and for making change. So we circulated promissory notes promising the buckskins were collectible when wanted. Meanwhile the hide was cleaned, scraped, tanned, dried, and stored.

However, when we substituted the convenient paper dollar, we had to trust the issuer that somewhere in storage or in the market there was an actual buckskin or other product of real worth for which the paper dollar could be exchanged.

It is no different today; for a paper dollar to be worth a dollar, there must be an equivalent value of goods produced somewhere for which the paper may be exchanged. But we are printing more paper IOUs without producing more buckskins. Somebody comes up short.

On the frontier we developed forty-three paper currencies, making them easy to counterfeit.

John Bogus came up before a frontier circuit judge in Ashtabula, Ohio, on a charge of counterfeiting. Hearing both plaintiff and defendant, the judge dismissed the case. After court the plaintiff berated the judge, "The bills were so obviously fake, how could you dismiss?"

"That's why. Nobody could possibly mistake them for bonafide dollars; therefore they are technically *not* counterfeit."

John Bogus's name came to mean obviously fake. The key is *obviously*.

Today, we are using dollars so *obviously* debased in buying power that they are not considered counterfeit. And the printer is getting off as free as John Bogus, printing these non-dollars on such an astounding scale we can't really believe it until we see the high-speed rotary inflation machines speeding us into dependency, poverty, and tyranny. Financial journalist James P. Gannon looked into why you must find a way, figuratively, to put milling on your paper money to protect you from your best enemy.

Your Multi-Billion Dollar Shaving Machine

There are armed guards in and around the pressroom at the Bureau of Engraving in Washington to prevent shoplifting, but they do not stop the machines from stealing from *us*. You will now see how *much* they are stealing.

Attention young people: These machines are committing large chunks of your future paychecks for years to come.

At the time of Mr. Gannon's visit to the Bureau of Engraving, printing foreman Arthur Baron was supervisor of the work there, standing amid a dozen belt-high skid loads of partly printed treasury bills. Treasury bills are IOUs. Each small bound package, no thicker than a ream of office stationery, was $300 million worth of IOUs.

"Those machines over there," Mr. Baron pointed out to Mr. Gannon, "used to be printing currency, but now we have them working pretty steadily on the debt."

The debt—you can tell by the casual phrasing—is already institutionalized in the language of Washington. It has lost the meaning "money owed." Why not? It is not expected to be repaid at anything like face value, not by the older generation. The younger generation will pay—and the generation after that.

The machines are printing those green, blue, and purple engravings at the stupefying rate of $1.5 billion a week. Much of the money thus borrowed (by selling these IOU treasury bills) is for vast federal aid programs where it will be, not invested, but consumed. There's a major difference: Money *invested* increases productivity, cuts inflation. Money consumed—that is, eaten, worn, drunk, or wasted—inflates prices.

Since Uncle Sam pays the most attractive interest in the

money market, these treasury bills will siphon dollars *away* from savings banks, stocks, and bonds, the usual money sources from which industry borrows to grubstake new machines to make *real* jobs and increase productivity, which in turn cuts inflation.

So the chief deflationary force, productive industry, is squeezed out of the play because it cannot compete with these treasury bills for the investor's dollar. Uncle Sam does not need to worry about how much interest he offers. He can outbid everybody in the big money auction because he is not going to pay the interest. You are. From taxation of your future earnings.

Now, back to Mr. Baron (or whoever may have succeeded him by now).

As his flood of newly printed treasury bills becomes additional money for the government to spend (and pay for at high interest), no equivalent in new buckskins or other products have been added. Therefore the new money instantly dilutes the value of the money already sitting in your wallet without even taking it out of your pocket. It dilutes the money in your savings account or safety deposit box without needing a key. It dilutes your future pension fund and your insurance policy.

Hence, what Mr. Baron is really printing is a tremendous new hidden tax on you without instruction from you or even your knowledge. The government is shaving the money. This is taxation without representation, a giant step back to tyranny.

Studies by the United Nations show that of the forty nations whose rates of inflation exceeded 15 percent from 1968 through 1972, thirty-eight abandoned the rules of democracy in favor of military junta or other form of dictatorship.[1]*

At this moment, the great underreported news story is the accelerating erosion of American liberty through use of a surprise weapon, government-sponsored inflation.

Memo to Youth: In regaining your freedom, controlling inflation is your critical move.

Inflation turns a nation around philosophically:
- from savers to spenders
- from producers to consumers

*Footnotes in this chapter and in chapter 9 are at end of chapters.

- ultimately from free men to welcomers of absolute government control.

Government must finally forcibly allocate all resources when debased currency will no longer do that.

No reader needs a definition of inflation. But to lick it (yes, it can be done), we need to know and understand the shocker— the United States government is chief inflator.

Watch.

Within days of Mr. Baron's explaining The Debt's printing machines, two other interesting events happened nearby. Down the hall from then Treasury Secretary Simon's office, a precocious thirty-five-year-old treasury man, Mr. Forbes, was worrying about the following no-win situation. Those IOUs which Mr. Baron was printing, Mr. Forbes had to sell as fast as they came off the presses. In other words, he and his colleagues had to borrow about $150 billion[2] in a year and a half. He was not worried that he would fail. He would make it. But being a trained and sensitive young economist, he knew that to borrow that much, he would out-compete corporations who wanted to attract the very same money to grubstake new factories, which step up productivity and thus depress inflation and create jobs.

Forbes knew his own activity would raise industry's interest costs and that many would be crowded out. Plant expansions would be cancelled, and new jobs.

He would compete with the young couples who want to borrow mortgage money to build homes, again reducing productivity and employment, increasing inflation on everything from townhouses to tomatoes. Still worse, Mr. Forbes knew Uncle Sam would pay back many of those IOUs by merely having Mr. Baron print more. So the lenders who received the government's high interest that year would be paid back later in printed money with still less buying power. Nobody would win but the government.

Welcome to big time inflation.

While Mr. Forbes was sweating out this one, his boss, the treasury secretary, explained to the House Budget Committee that "unprecedented government borrowing is draining funds from housing and business investment," thus throttling the hoped-for economic upturn in capital intensive industries.

No more than a thousand yards from that meeting, other treasury officials were asking Congress for another increase in the federal debt limit ceiling. They needed to borrow not $50 billion but $80 billion, they said. At that time the total federal debt was already $544 billion. Just paying the interest on that debt was costing $36 billion per year, the government's third largest budget item, right behind welfare and national defense.

In the three weeks astride these events, the *Wall Street Journal* reported corporations canceling $700 million worth of plant expansion bond offerings that would have created real jobs, more productivity, and reduced inflation.

The House Budget Committee complimented the secretary on his lucid warning but nevertheless approved raising the debt limit. Publicly the House of Representatives generally votes as if they believe massive federal aid to the least productive parts of society has a better chance of sparking an economic upturn than investment money flowing to productive industry. Privately, of course, they know that trying to spend our way out of inflation is like drinking ourselves sober. But the hangover won't hit *their* generation. It's the younger generation who will suffer.

Mr. Baron received his instruction to step up production on The Debt. Shave the currency.

As parents, we can have no joy, knowing this government is not sufficiently lasting to ensure anything which we may bequeath to posterity.
—Common Sense

Under this system, Uncle Sam's spending *per household*, according to Tax Foundation estimates a couple years ago, exceeded a rate of $9,960 per year. By now the figure is higher.

That does not shock the citizen...because he doesn't know it. But on the heels of that comes news of the biggest budget coverup in history—"off-budget accounting." The Watergate coverup pales by comparison.

William Simon informs us in *A Time for Truth* how this hidden debt builds. "Politicians discovered that they could launch federal programs and win the enthusiastic support of grateful voters without taking a penny out of the Treasury."

The government simply *replaced old bonds with new ones* as debts fell due. Thus, many forms of debt do not show up in the budget, including price support programs and a number of different social welfare programs, except perhaps as footnotes describing them as "off-budget."

And so we continue to proliferate recorded and unrecorded debt faster than our ability to pay.[3]

However, balancing the national budget during recession years is difficult and undesirable. The tax load required makes recessions more severe.

A negative income tax, as suggested in Chapter 3, would provide the very great advantage of automatically (and not by intervention of the huge government bureaucracy) adding much needed purchasing power during periods of low economic activity, decreasing the severity of recessions.

To avoid inflation, it is of course necessary during years of economic recovery to create a surplus to again bring the budget into balance.

Increasing taxes during years of recession is much like the old practice of bleeding sick people to cure them. George Washington was bled heavily four times during his last illness and never recovered. Modern medical practice is to add blood infusions as needed, drawing from blood banks accumulated from healthy, compassionate donors. The nation's financial health during difficult and good times requires similar treatment.

But this does not cancel the basic law of economics, which eludes sophisticated government financial counselors but is very clear to nearly every housewife: "*The thing about debt . . . sooner or later somebody's got to pay.*"

Only big government could be so oblivious to the obvious.

Government creates inflation many other ways. Staggering bureaucratic burden raises prices, but at least it is visible. Obscene government waste is inflationary, but it is partly visible. Tremendous counterproductive and inflationary government regulation, adding $200 billion to consumer prices, are partly visible.

These are stupefying inflationary costs. But the really staggering threat is from the *hidden* taxing power of Mr. Baron's rotary inflation machines shaving the currency.

Get your friends to feel the edge of a quarter and ask them why the ridges. Then tell them.

When a great democracy's money fails, the democracy falls.

"Then Freeze Prices?"

Brilliant leaders, economic advisers, and politicians ultimately back into this last fall-back trench, always to be stunned by the ensuing boomerang.

Funny thing about money—price controls reduce production and can raise prices.

Why?

Prices are a language.

They talk to us.

Freeze them, and we can't hear their message.

A newscast warning of an approaching hurricane is bad news, but we're better off having that bad news. Freezing prices censors the news that prices are trying to tell us; it does not stop the inflation hurricane.

What are the messages?

- That certain shortages sneaking up on us need our attention.
- That we are paying ourselves more than we are earning (low productivity and resultant shortages).
- That we are not saving enough (for investing in more productive machinery).
- That most of all, in the words of the nation's sharp-tongued Dutch uncle, Citibank Chairman Walter Wriston, "the government has printed too much money (...) since 1967 the government has caused the money supply to grow three times as fast as the goods and services that can be bought with it." That bids up prices.

Freeze prices and none of these messages gets through, yet the hurricane continues building even though we have switched off the warning newscast.

Freezing prices drives inflation underground. For example, during one Russian inflation, farmers abandoned currency and accepted rubies for small bags of potatoes. Next stage: When trading jewelry is gone, robbery and riots. People fight for the potatoes.

No army of inspectors is large enough to control prices. The weak cannot compete for food in the black market; the strong battle for necessities, creating anarchy.

Now pause thirty seconds to ask yourself what the government must do next.

If it cannot control prices, *it must switch over to controlling the resources.* It cannot let the black market decide who shall eat.

The government must move in as allocator of everything—decide who shall get what and how much of it.

At that moment good-bye, personal liberty. "Because," as Wriston points out, "government allocation of economic resources requires force." Economic freedom is at the base of all freedoms. "To think that the bell does not toll for academic freedom or freedom of the press if economic freedom is shackled is dangerous illusion."

A whole generation now reaches age twenty-five not even knowing its own enormous loss of liberty.

"Suppose we're willing to swap liberty for deflation, what's wrong with price controls?"

Well. . .crazy thing about price controls, they create unforeseen results, some good, some bad.

By jamming the economic signals they delay solutions by hordes of imaginative, inventive people among our 230 million. For example, the rising price of jogging shoes signaled an unemployed new college graduate that the time was ripe for a sports shoe retreading business. In his first month he was deluged. Today scores of such shops across the country are suddenly retreading sports shoes that once were junked.

Perry Mendel, a former real estate man in Montgomery, Alabama, noted that working mothers paid sharply rising prices for daytime sitters. That was a message to Mendel. Why couldn't prices be brought down and more useful activities for the kids result from some kind of group sitting? He invested $15,000 to start Kinder-Care Learning Center, Inc. Today Kinder-Care is in twenty-three states, charging reasonable rates, taking good care of 22,000 kids. It has spawned competition, creating a large new industry.

Young Ted C. Wetterau's family were grocers in Hazelwood,

Missouri. He watched the public abandon their favorite local independent grocery stores because prices were lower in the big chain outlets. Family grocers were closing up shop, ending a friendly social institution. Wetterau decided to furnish for independent grocers the same kind of economical wholesale warehousing operation enjoyed by the chains. It worked like a charm. Independents, using Wetterau's wholesale warehouses, could lower their prices, retain their customers, and keep the local feel. Young Wetterau's warehouse business has grown to $832 million annual volume.

Price controls hide the vital signals that bring out of the woods millions of capable people with imaginative solutions for inflationary shortages. From unfrozen rising prices came plastic construction piping, liquid nail fasteners, paperback books, and. . .ultimately *falling prices*.

Memo to the Future: Let prices give you their true messages and trigger the ingenuity of a population containing more precocious minds and specialized knowledge than any government can muster.

Price controls hide the need for ingenious low cost alternatives and thus propagate inflation.

The secret economy. Both inflation and price controls drive trade underground.

Even in the bondage of price controls, the former free market still struggles to tell us the true market values, no matter who is trying to control them. For example, while OPEC tried to maintain a price of $34 per barrel for oil, a huge subsurface oil spot market developed. During the period of shortage, customers were willing to pay $40 per barrel, and did so.

Every industry does it. Banks, not content with controlled interest rates, lend their funds where they can acquire fringes, extra points, or equity in the borrower's operation. Under price controls, stores reduce services, which is a way of raising prices.

A big market also develops in untraceable, untaxable cash and barter. Many estimate this trade at $200 billion per year already, an enormous portion of the nation's total business.

Uncontrolled inflation develops still another type of underground economy. A widow, Mattie Shultz, aged ninety-one, walked out of a San Antonio food store empty-handed. That in itself alerted store personnel, but besides that, she wore a raincoat on a Texas-hot day. When they stopped her she had $15 worth of ham and sausage under the raincoat.

Her simple defense reached the headlines, "I was desperate hungry."

A sympathetic, inflation-weary public sent her food and money. Mattie Shultz is the opposite side of the giant spot market coin.

Dramatic rises in shoplifting sync neatly with inflation step-ups.

Wall Street Journal writer Bill Abrams estimated that the holiday heist from just November 26 to December 24, 1979, was $1.6 billion. "People are looking for ways to beat inflation." Stuart Tomesky of the Fooderama chain in New York and New Jersey reports, "You catch people who never dreamed of stealing three years ago."

Two retailer associations estimate that shoplifting losses of about $8 billion a year are passed on to the paying customers. That's more inflation.

Controls can dam the inflation waters until they build overwhelming pent-up power. Then the dam bursts —there's defiant shoplifting, a black market, a spot market, strikes, and finally price rises. The cycle continues at a new higher level.

A new generation of government men then comes to power with a great new idea, "Let's freeze prices."

Who, but big government, would be so oblivious to the obvious—you don't put a lid on a boiling kettle to cool it?

Unlimited competition is the finest type of price control.

Voluntary citizen price control? Actually, we citizens often think we are fighting against inflation when instead we are *hedging* against it. That is totally different. We have learned not to hold dollars. They shrink. So if we need a car *next* year, we buy it *now* to beat inflation.

And so inflation breeds inflation.

The incentive is against saving that money. Simple arithmetic. Inflation shrinks our savings by more than the bank pays us in interest. Laughably, our government then *taxes* that interest as if it were profit. Yet if we had borrowed instead of saving, our government would have allowed a tax deduction on our interest cost. So if a man has the nerve and the brains, during inflation he does not save, he borrows.

And he does not save, he spends.

In the worst case on record, post-World War I Germany, employees were paid daily so they could spend Monday's pay before it devalued on Tuesday. Later they were paid twice daily; money was shrinking hourly.

Ask people to voluntarily cease hedging against inflation? Over two thousand years of experience say it will not work.

So? Throw in the Towel on America?

The steps that follow are widely agreed upon by leading economists as a sure modus operandi for slowing inflation.

How is not the question. But *who*?

Hired government will not voluntarily cut its own inflationary size, unproductivity, nor waste. It is not capable of increasing productivity. It is not motivated to stop overdrawing its account and issuing excess money.

So who can do it?

The multi-term veteran congressional incumbent? He knows the correct course, but the full disaster won't occur until *after* his retirement from office. Why should he risk political defeat by opposing the continuing inflationary transfer of funds from the most productive element of society to the least productive, which has the most voters. The veteran political incumbent will not vote for pain in his precinct.

Industry? Industry can accomplish many things, but not inflation control. If the professional manager pays escalating prices for raw materials and does not raise his own selling price, he is only months from bankruptcy. Long before that he is fired.

The investor? We've already seen that the investor, properly seeking shelter from inflation, compounds inflation. Dismiss him.

If none of these can execute the inflation control program, who is left?

We must reach way back to Tom Paine's *Common Sense* to find the figure who has forgotten his most important identity—the citizen-as-government.

Some convenient tree will afford them a State House, under the branches of which, the whole colony may assemble to deliberate on public matters. In this first parliament every man, by natural right, will have a seat.
— Common Sense

Unfortunately, that's us. We've shed our role gradually over two hundred years, becoming by default the citizen-as-subject, allowing our hired deputy to become our boss.

The qualified voter must fire his present deputies and take up his duties as government. It may be too late. The two-minute warning blew and we're out of time-outs.

But big government cannot exist without a big vote and big taxes. Therefore, if we have the intelligence and the concern, we must seek, find, put forward, and elect across the entire slate from village to federal, candidates who promise us the least help and the most common sense.

Can we do this? Yes. How?

Join us in Chapter 8.

Meanwhile, what financial steps will work?

The Care and Handling of Inflation

Oblivious to the obvious, like a bird in a room, we're free to escape but can't see the open window.

"*I want my raise.*" Those four words bomb mass citizen enthusiasm for inflation control.

But there are two ways to get a raise. The first—increase the paycheck. That raise will soon be wiped out by inflation. The second is to *increase the value of the dollar.* That gives us a raise we can keep.

So first, stop talking about reducing inflation, and start talking about *raising the buying power of the dollar. That gives everybody a raise that does not melt before we get it home.*

Raising the purchasing power of a dollar may become complex when you get down to daily tactics, but viewed from the mountain top the long-range strategy is simple:

- By real incentives, encourage saving (which buys machinery, which increases productivity, which increases the purchasing power of the dollar).
- Eliminate destructive government interference and regulation (which will quickly increase productivity, reduce scarcity, and thus increase the purchasing power of your dollar).
- Discourage inflationary government spending (and the resultant creation of new dollars to dilute the value of your dollar).

These actions would give us all a raise by increasing the value of a dollar.

Is It Possible?

Yes, past history proves the point.

"Sound as a dollar," has become meaningless now that a fifty-dollar bill hardly pays for a trip to the grocery.

Believe it or not, however, five dollars would have purchased about the same bag of groceries *for most of the first 150 years of U. S. existence.*

Actually, although slightly inflated, even at the end of World War II the dollar was the world's most valuable currency. At that time, you could hardly find customers in a foreign country who had dollars and could pay for U.S. exports. It was not easy. Many U.S. companies were forced to manufacture abroad to be able to sell for those foreign currencies. One of your authors did just that. The solution was a factory in Scotland, selling over a large part of the world for British sterling.

Now Europeans, Asians, and Arabs have our dollars stuffed into every pocket. These are called Euro-dollars.

What is behind that old saying "sound as a dollar"? To finance the Revolutionary War, the Continental Congress issued paper dollars known as *continentals*, backed mostly by patriotic hope. Before long they became a symbol for worthless—"not worth a continental."

In the late 1700s, the U.S. dollar was minted in silver and then the paper dollar was issued, backed by gold, solving our newly formed democracy's currency problem. And it remained solved for 140 years (until the 1930s). The United States went off the gold standard in 1933.

Now let us take a quick look at how our "sound U.S. dollar"

acted over that whole 140 years. In 1790, one sound dollar (of the value arbitrarily selected by the authors) would purchase about $1.50 worth of goods. (We'll explain that in a moment.) In the early 1800s, the War of 1812 had to be financed. The purchasing power of our sound dollar dropped very briefly to around seventy-five cents. Then, as a result of our industrious forefathers producing and watching over government expenditures, it wasn't very long before our sound dollar was purchasing a $1.50 market basket.

This excellent valuable dollar continued its high purchasing power until the Civil War. Again, the Civil War had to be financed. This lowered the purchasing power of the sound dollar briefly again to approximately seventy-five cents.

But, again, Americans were excellent producers and good watch dogs over government expenditures, so, as before, one sound U.S. dollar soon was able to buy about $1.50 worth of goods.

This value continued, with only minor variations, through the Spanish-American War until World War I. As in previous major wars, the value of our sound dollar then dropped, this time to about seventy cents. Again, during the 1920s, high productivity and low government costs resulted in the beginning of the recovery of our dollar's purchasing power, but this time reaching only about eighty cents by 1929. Full recovery from World War I was aborted by the 1929-1940 depression.[4]

The value arbitrarily selected by the authors for the "Sound U.S. Dollar" is the approximate average for the period of 1790 to 1930 of the U.S. Labor Department's C.P.I. (Consumer Price Index).

The somewhat futile attempts to end the 1930s depression, compounded by World War II, dropped the purchasing power of our dollar to about fifty cents by around 1950. With productivity rising more slowly and government expenditures rising enormously as a result of the Korean and Vietnam wars, the purchasing power of our once-sound dollar fell by 1981 to roughly ten cents. And it's lost additional value since then.

That is the story. Hence we are now spending more than $50.00 to purchase a $5.00 market basket of groceries.

Could we win back our sound U.S. dollar? Yes.

First, we must produce smarter (not necessarily harder). A good way is to stimulate creative initiative and benefit by the incentive of the 20/20 plan for saving (See Chapter 3).

Second, demonstrate real concern for the well-being of others, either by providing money or effort or both, not just lip service. Again the 20/20-plan incentive for contribution to charity described in Chapter 3 will go far toward accomplishing just this.

Third, reduce government—federal, state and local—to minimums.

Fourth, closely, thoroughly, and persistently monitor our progress towards the objective of a 100-cent *Sound American Dollar.*

This will take a long period of time and much effort, but it does not need to cause severe hardships.

Assuming we, the voting citizens, can increase the purchasing power of our present dollar by 8 percent per year for five years, we will increase its true value from the 1981 ten cents to 14.7 cents. This would be a 47 percent increase. Not a bad raise, and in real buying power. Eight percent per year for five years should not be difficult. The savings in interest cost from the existing high rates down to a true rate of 2 percent to 3 percent, added to immediate reduction in some of big government's cost should accomplish much of this first five-year savings target, with a good possibility gains would be much higher than 8 percent.

A next reasonable objective seems to be to raise purchasing power 5 percent per year for ten years, making the dollar at the end of fifteen years worth 23.9 cents true value. Now we have a 139 percent real increase, again a very nice increase in real buying power.

After this, since raising the purchasing power further will probably be more difficult, lower the estimated yearly target rate of increase to 3 percent. Milton Friedman on page 191 of *Free to Choose* notes there was a 3 percent per year increase in output per man-hour of all persons employed in private business in the twenty-year period from 1949 to 1969, substantiating the achievability of the target rate. Using this rate for an additional twenty-four years, the purchasing power of our dollar will have recovered by year 2020 to fifty cents, a 400 percent increase in purchasing power as compared to the 1981 ten-cent value.

Many of us will still be alive in year 2020, some at retirement age, when we will appreciate the sound dollar.

Continuing on at the 3 percent yearly increase in productivity, the full value of our sound American dollar would be restored in a total of sixty-two years (the year 2043). That would be a tremendous real increase in pay and in living standards for everyone.

Many of you will be alive in 2043 to enjoy it; and you will have given your children a powerful heritage—a sound dollar. This is probably the only nation which still has a chance politically to achieve this.

Mechanization and automation will accomplish this increased purchasing power of our sound dollar without reduced wages except for products or services requiring a large amount of labor. As an example, in agriculture 2.8 percent of our population feeds the nation, as compared to about 80 percent at the time of Tom Paine.

Necessities of life, including education, should become lower in price as related to wages. The other necessity of shelter—and luxury items or services with a high labor content—can be expected to remain high-priced, since wages are expected to remain near present rates. Also, the increasing shortages of many low cost raw material resources make the United States dependent on more higher cost sources.

The figures the U.S. Labor Department uses to determine the progress being made back towards the 1790-1930 sound dollar should include only cost-of-living items that are comparable to those items in that base 140-year period. Apples should be compared to apples; that is common sense. Perhaps these monitoring figures should be called the N.P.I. (Necessity Price Index).

When the stable "sound as a dollar" money (based on monitoring of the N.P.I.) has been achieved, our free market economy will then be able to raise wages still further in acceptable increments in sync with rises sparked by a worldwide free market competitive environment.

Further, at that time, it would be common sense to consider

returning to the gold standard to assure sustaining a full-value sound dollar.

A lot of people will scoff—"The authors are dreamers. These are simplistic, impossible visions, pie in the sky."

So Look at the Alternative

The alternative is continued confiscatory inflation. Then in a generation, say thirty-five years, the ten-cent dollar will have buying power of about one-third of one cent, based on the "sound American dollar."[5]

About that same time, in the year 2020, following the common sense plan just outlined, the "sound American dollar" would have recovered to fifty cents.

One alternative is a disaster, the other a slow but good recovery. When our young children are about forty years old, will they have a fifty-cent dollar or a dollar worth one-third of one cent? If the former, they will be free citizens; if the latter, they will be government wards. They won't have had a voice in the decision.

It is your choice—now.

But How Do We Get Started?

What we are basically proposing on a national scale is the same two things your common sense has been doing if you are running a farm or business or household—decrease the expenses, increase the productivity. Common sense.

Let's slide in easy, so as not to get the natives too agitated. Are you ready?

1. Pay your own taxes.

Question: How much is your federal income tax on a biweekly basis?

You don't know without looking it up, right?

Neither do most of us. Thus, the biggest single cost we pay every payday is the best-kept secret from us. That's what put us to sleep in the first place. We don't fully realize we work from January to May entirely for the government.

A powerful first step that can be made is to change the law so that every taxpayer must personally pay his own income taxes. Write the check yourself. Revoke the payroll deduction method.

The screams from Washington will shatter the windows in Tulsa. Don't listen. Insist upon it. "Look, we're not asking for lower taxes with this law. We simply want to scrap payroll deduction. Every income taxpayer must pay his own taxes."

That is a reasonable proposition. It asks no favors. It deprives no government agency. Certainly it increases the cost of collecting taxes. But that will be cheap.

If every taxpayer had to sit down every three months and write his own surprising large check for his own taxes, inflation would be on the way out. The citizen would have taken a massive step back to taking charge of his government.

Every quarter when the taxpayer sits down to write his check to pay for his government, he will have a new interest in what he bought for that money. The answers will enrage him. He will probably decide he didn't want to work to pay $732 million for defaulted student loans. The citizen will talk to his neighbors about it. He will suddenly notice his government employee neighbors and ask what they do that is important enough to warrant this huge tax bill.

The citizen will probably decide he doesn't want to pay for mass jet fly-overs for general officers' retirement parties, subsidize lame duck congressmen's trip to Micronesia, or pay for a huge government publishing house he never uses. When he writes his own income tax check, it will be hard to convince him he should automatically send foreign aid to 191 nations without receiving from his congressman any explanation or report of these loans and gifts.

Suddenly, every time a Chicago congressman votes for a money bill contributing to an art museum in New York, he will consider that bill less in light of what he owes the congressman from New York and more in the light of what he owes his constituents in Chicago.

It will take some years to remove the payroll-deduction method of collecting income taxes, including endless court tests.

But start now. It can be done.

2. Stop eating the seed corn. Unleash the productive creativity of industry as quickly as possible to step up productivity. For quickest results, stop eating the seed money.

Funny thing about money, there are two distinct types—seed money and eating money (capital and consumption). They should be totally different colors. Eating money is fun; you can drink it, waste it, tax it, or spend it on wild parties and it won't hurt you much.

Seed money is something else. It is very exciting. It is growth money. When you plant it, the most amazing magic occurs for everyone involved. But if you ever get caught eating the seed money, spending it for consumption items, your future is dead.

Seed money is the money industry uses to buy the machines that create the jobs. This kind of money steps up production, reduces shortages, raises the buying power of the dollar. This is the kind of money that wise old men mean when they tell their kids, "You can buy all the hot cars and horses you want from your interest income, but never, never, never live off your capital!"

However, government has diverted huge amounts of seed money to massive aid programs, converting it to consumption money. Consumption money builds no factories. The way to get this seed money back is to foster tax policies that encourage saving and investing.

At present the U.S. citizen is saving a smaller percent of his disposable income than his counterpart in any other large industrial nation. There's a reason. Current U.S. tax policy makes it stupid to save.

Encourage saving by a tax policy that stops making the saver an idiot. Japan not only refrains from taxing interest on savings, it gives the saver bonuses.

Give the small business guy freedom. Eliminate *all* reporting for employers of under ten persons. No forms to fill out; no tax accountant needed. Employment will multiply.

Encourage business investment incentives. Kill the triple-dip corporation income tax.

Even the most accomplished sneak thief would have trouble picking three pockets at the same time. But big government's corporation income tax does just that. Here's how.

The first dip: The corporation is taxed on its profit. Inflation increases this dip. After that tax, part of the remaining profit is paid to the stockholders as dividends to pay them for the use of their money and for their risk.

The second dip: The stockholders now pay income taxes on these dividends, which have already been taxed once as corporate profit. Don't forget that a lot of these taxed dividends go to a special kind of stockholder, the workmen's pension funds. This second dip hits them.

The third dip: The public (including the stockholders and workers) pay again because corporations pass on their tax expense to the public. More inflation.

Incidentally, notice the incentive for corporate waste: Why not a three-martini lunch, since government pays nearly half the check—it's triply tax-deductible.

Eliminating the triple-dip corporation income tax would:
- make U.S. products more competitive in world markets, increasing exports, improving U.S. balance of payments;
- increase employment;
- reduce corporate waste;
- decrease prices;
- increase capital expenditures;
- make the United States a stronger nation.

Income taxes must be paid directly, obviously, and honestly (not in hidden form) by tax-paying citizens, not by taxing a piece of paper called a corporation. Corporation income taxes (on productive corporations approved for exemption by the Internal Revenue Service) must be abolished.

This action will turn a stream of seed money back into refurbishing our outmoded U.S. factory, creating more productivity, which raises the value of the dollar.

This step will be difficult, yet easier than some others because at this writing there is a hopeful shift of attitudes toward tax laws favoring saving and capital formation for new machinery.

The sentiment is there, but it needs an all-out boost by the mass voice of the citizen government.

Peter F. Drucker, in *Forbes* magazine, May 23, 1983, comparing the two great economists Joseph A. Schumpeter and Maynard Keynes, observed that Schumpeter's economic development..."makes profit fulfill an economic function...." Capital formation and productivity are needed to maintain the wealth-producing capacity of the economy and, above all, to maintain today's jobs and to create tomorrow's jobs.

3. Shut the bureau drawers. Do this slowly at first to keep down the screams. Later, we'll slam the bureau drawers shut. But start quietly.

Release the fuller productivity of our nation of creative workers by getting the stultifying interference of regulatory bureaus out of our factories. Mr. Murphy, when chairman of General Motors, reported a cost of $1.3 billion for his company alone to comply with government regulations.

Certainly some supervision of industry for the security of the people is a function of government—when we ask for it. Business has just as many bad guys as any other sector. But the tragic destruction of the productivity of the once greatest industrial nation by swarms of uninformed interfering bureaucrats in the nation's workplace is killing us. The terrible loss in productivity is compounded by the addition of an estimated $130 billion of *unnecessary* dead weight cost passed on to the customer.

Relief from that alone would make our dollar instantly worth a lot more.

Closing the bureau drawer may not be too hard to achieve. The country is ready. (See Chapter 8.)

4. Fire Aunt Samantha. Our nation contains strong creative individuals. Free them from Aunt Samantha, who is replacing Uncle Sam and bringing in the concept of government as den mother.

Here is the design and end of government, viz, freedom and security.
—Common Sense

But big Samantha is training a softening populace to think government should warm our milk, test our Dr. Dentons for flammability, protect us from poison ivy, strap us in our cars, study the sweetener in our coffee—and at fantastic cost. That is not hired government's role.

Certainly we want government to protect the deprived. But deprived does not mean the child who doesn't have piano lessons nor the college student who doesn't have steaks.

Let our volunteer organizations take care of moderate troubles and as much deprivation as they can. It is better for our character and it is cheaper. Save government for catastrophic misfortune.

Massive den-mother programs render the people helpless, discourage private welfare in which we take care of each other, and dilute our dollar in oceans of waste. The ingenuity of the people can solve problems with street wisdom and concern for each other, preserving self-reliance.

The time is right. There is a growing impatience with the den mother's swine flu comedy, cyclamate foul ups, and the annual multibillion-dollar bungle.

If Samantha were a nice old lady that might be one thing, but since the job became so lush, she's more often a porcelain-eyed twenty-eight-year-old MBA driving a Datsun XL250; and anything she ever gave us, she had to swipe from us first. She should be fired.

Cutting back her cumbersome programs will free funds to do a real job for the truly needy, who often get shouldered aside in present welfare programs.

5. Reinstate the great daily referendum. To raise the value of the dollar, let competition have at it. That is the swiftest price control.

At 11:15 A.M., November 8, 1979, twenty-seven-year-old W. J. Bedford, manager, Rego's Grocery on Center Ridge Road, Westlake, Ohio, walked into his store. Something didn't look right.

By this time in the morning the packaged dinners department should be a mess from shoppers pawing through the stock. But it was neat. He said to the department manager, "Jim, did you just straighten shelves?"

"No. Been neat all morning."

"What's the matter?"

"Heinen's is featuring packaged dinners in their west side stores. Two 7$\frac{1}{4}$oz. Kraft Macaroni and Cheese for sixty-nine cents."

Bedford went to his mezzanine office looking down over the six checkout lanes and watched for five minutes. Very few packaged dinners going through. He phoned Jim some instructions.

By 11:45 A.M., Jim was remarking Rego's macaroni and cheese shelf, "Two (7$\frac{1}{4}$ oz.) Pkgs. 67¢."

Besides Kraft Macaroni & Cheese 7$\frac{1}{4}$oz. dinners, Bedford has 6,000 items in his store. He watches daily, sometimes hourly, how the people going through his six checkout voting booths are voting on his prices. And he reacts immediately.

Multiply that by every industry, every city and town, every

product. By this hourly vote, the people influence prices of hundreds of thousands of products with lightning speed.

Now substitute for that a government attempt to monitor and control prices. Even with an army of inspectors, can you see how they could possibly monitor and control even the prices of just the 113 brands and types of shampoo (dry, normal, and oily) in all the stores in the three-thousand U.S. counties? We would drown in the paperwork. And ultimately price controls may raise prices. By squelching normal price rises, they kill the motive for innovators to invent lower-cost substitutes.

Over the long run, the great cash register referendum tends to lower prices. Let it work.

6. Go private. Don't try this until you get a good start on the others; but for tremendous gains in the value of your dollar gradually transfer from government to private industry as many services as feasible. While we looked at that in Chapter 1 as a way of improving services, here we're looking at it as a tremendous way of improving the buying power of your dollar.

The present huge costs and poor productivity are not the government's fault. By the nature of government it *cannot* run a business productively or profitably. But it *can* act as purchasing agent and supervisor of private contractor performance with respect to:

- school buses
- mail
- water supply
- rubbish collection

- building operations
- dam construction
- military post exchanges
- road maintenance

Dr. Paul P. Salaberren, the minister of economy for Buenos Aires Province, Argentina, brought the enormous provincial budget into balance in four years, despite savage inflation, by wholesale return of public operations to private industry. "There is no worse businessman than the government," he says smilingly. "We have sold 3,200 large and small government properties to the private sector and are constantly converting others. For instance, in the Hippodrome of La Plata, which belonged to the provincial government, we had 5,000 employees. We leased it to a private organization, and now we have only eight supervisory employees there."

Making this conversion will be difficult because of entrenched agencies with entrenched support. But we could start small.

Rural-Metro, the fire department in Scottsdale, Arizona, is privately owned. The fire trucks, for instance, are plain basic trucks. They cost about $28,000 each, compared to an estimated $40,000-$70,000 for one of the conventional chrome-spangled fire trucks.

Louis Witzeman, Rural-Metro owner, knows that if his charges to the city are excessive he will be replaced. So he has no chrome polishers or men sitting around waiting for alarms. If they aren't fighting fires, they're building or rebuilding the fire trucks or working on some other innovation such as a robot to carry the hose into the heart of the blaze, installing larger than conventional hose, or challenging some other tradition.

Chief Witzeman says, "Tradition is one of the biggest things screwing up the fire-fighting business."

The $880,000 cost to Scottsdale is considered less than half the cost of a conventional department.

Scottsdale is a microscopic example, but multiply that across the nation and project it to all other contractable services.

7. Restore sound money. Sound money must have responsible backing. Two obvious choices are:

- •. A responsible government operating within responsible guidelines.
- •. Or currency fully backed by precious metals, making government financially responsible.

A combination of both seems a common-sense solution. Between 1934, when private ownership of gold in the United States was prohibited (the beginning of big inflation and big government) and 1978, when gold ownership by individuals was again permitted, this could not have been done.

Now the United States is minting half-ounce and one-ounce gold coins as medallions. Citizens can now monitor the purchasing power of our paper dollar in terms of gold simply by asking the dollar price of a medallion. A phone call will do it. The Post Office has a toll-free hot line so you can find out prices of gold coins daily.

This monitoring allows steps to be taken to keep the dollar recovery plan on target.

After the sound dollar of 1790-1930 has been reached, it

seems best to adopt the gold standard. To progress to that point, it is common sense just to monitor the progress towards achieving that goal. With no gold standard, the only restraint against inflation is public opinion.

8. Shut down Mr. Baron's printing press. Every economist quickly states that the first common-sense requisite for controlling inflation is for the government to stop creating money at a rate that exceeds national productivity.

So why have we put it last?

Because the only way we will get any government to stop creating excess money is to reduce the costs of government. That is what the preceding seven moves will do.

When the United States can once again sell securities yielding 2 or 3 percent interest, the true rate of interest, citizens will know inflation no longer exists.

If these steps are implemented aggressively, purchasing power growth can soon take over from retrenchment, with greater security for all.

In 1981, the United States paid $50.00 for a market basket of necessities that could have been purchased for an average price of $5.00 during the 140-year period, 1790-1930. Raising our ten-cent dollar to fifty cents by the year 2020 is a reasonable possibility. Initial rates of recovery can be rapid through large early cost savings. Our resources to accomplish continued recovery are strong. Regaining the full (excluding luxury items) 100-cent dollar by the year 2043 (an additional twenty-three years) seems attainable by maintaining the 3 percent average annual increase in output that was accomplished during the period 1949 to 1969. Self-reliance, creative effort, and working smartly to achieve increased productivity of goods and services plus close monitoring of big government's expenditures should substantially shorten the sound dollar's recovery time.

It's common sense.

It Happened in Maine

They are going to tell you rising government costs cannot be turned around.

James B. Longley is a relatively young man with a face already lined by character and achievement in the insurance business. His hair is thinning some. His eyes are full of years, his pleasant smile is guarded by a blunt chin. He lives in Maine, and he has been thinking a lot about liberty and inflation.

Maine had always been a state of mind: self-reliance, pay your bills, a day's work for a day's pay. But suddenly the state had developed enormous debt, a monstrous welfare establishment, and unseemly eagerness for handouts.

James Longley, an amateur in politics, announced that he was running for governor of Maine on the promise that he would erase Maine's highest deficit in history without raising taxes; he would balance fiscal responsibility with humanitarianism. And he would serve only one term.

To the amazement of the professionals, he was elected.

He knew he was in for a rough time. But the day after inauguration, he called a cabinet meeting for 7:00 A.M. He told them to stop lobbying with legislators for their pet programs, cut all out-of-state travel, freeze all hiring, and, as incentive to state officials, pass the word that there would be no raises until the budget was in balance.

All agencies were to reduce spending 7 percent below approved budgets. State grants to towns for snow removal and such would cease. Towns would practice home rule and home service.

To set the pace, he cut his own salary to $20,000.

In four years, largely by attrition, Longley reduced the state payroll from 14,000 to 12,000.

He examined every application for federal funds personally and scrapped many. "We must stop misleading people into believing the government can give more than it takes."

Political opponents in the hostile legislature circulated rumors that Longley was suffering a nervous breakdown. Reporters dubbed him "El Wacko."

Resisting aggressive pressure groups was rougher than Longley expected, but he vetoed 109 money bills, 53 successfully.

He discovered the state's economic development department maintained nine offices and fifty-three staffers. He cut it to one office and nine staffers and enlisted the state's regular summer visitors into a volunteer corps, Friends of Maine. Their mission: set up appointments in their home states with top corporate executives for Maine's economic development people. Result: eighty-six companies expanded facilities into Maine, creating seventy-four new plants and 11,300 jobs.

Maine's welfare program was running away, swallowing one-third of the state's budget. Aid to Dependent Children alone threatened to mushroom to $130 million per year. Abuses were rampant. Longley instituted programs to recover support money from runaway fathers and to weed out the well-off food stamp recipients and ADC families.

Resistance was vindictive. But hardship payments were increased to the truly needy even as welfare payments across the board dropped dramatically. For example, ADC leveled off at $50 million.

As the 1978 election approached, Longley had become a legend. The press predicted he would be a 2 to 1 winner over any rival and urged him to run. Longley declined, keeping his one-term campaign promise.

John Martin, leader of the rival party, said, "Jim Longley finally made people realize that whatever they get from the government, they pay for."

We need a national cadre of Longleys. The authors' generation will not lick inflation for you. We started it.

So you are it.

Before you tackle Congress, however, you have a problem with your own young contemporaries. Their voting record is worse than ours.

Must they go through an economic Pearl Harbor before it will be acceptable to vote against inflation?

Show them the ridges on the quarters; tell them why they are needed for freedom—why a president must veto special interest (pork barrel) items—be held fully responsible for holding down big government's expenses—why the budget must be balanced.

As Ludwig von Mises stated in *Human Action*, "Continued inflation must finally end in the crack-up boom, the complete breakdown of the currency system.... Practically, the danger of deflation is but slight and the danger of inflation tremendous."

NOTES

1. Anthony Fisher in Vol. 3, *The Ludwig von Mises Lecture Series,* Hillsdale College Press, 1976.

2. The concept of a billion is very difficult. For congressmen, it is written without the nine zeros. So they forget. But a billion hours ago would take you back to the year 112,175 B.C. A billion dollars runs your federal government until about noon each day.

3. Additionally, in computing the national debt, we do not include debts of quasi-independent governmental agencies. TVA owes $11 billion. Federal Home Loan Board owes $88 billion. Federal Housing Administration, the VA, and Farmers Home Agency have guaranteed loans of $237 billion. There are others, bringing cumulative liabilities at this writing to at least $7.8 trillion or about $151,000 per taxpayer.

4. See *The Wall Street Journal,* November 11, 1980: "Inflation Zero 1792 to 1930s."

5. Estimated from the article on page 19 of *The Bank Credit Analyst,* November 1980.

6

MORE LIBERTY—
MORE HONESTY

Can It Happen Here?

Big government, big inflation, and big taxes add up to what?
CONKEY'S TAVERN, PELHAM, MASSACHUSETTS. Like the best
taverns everywhere, Conkey's was not only a place to join
friends, it was the area's political forum. Opinion was heated by
strong waters.

On one particular autumn evening there in Pelham, the heat
was compounded by anger at an arrogant government in Massachusetts causing big taxes and big inflation, impoverishing
farmers to the point of desperation.

What do desperate Americans do?

A long and violent abuse of power is generally the means of calling the
right of it in question. . . .

—Common Sense

Into Conkey's tavern came a delegation of men from several
towns quite distant from Pelham, looking for someone. They
stood inside the tavern door until their eyes adjusted to the
gloom, then walked directly to a table where a few friends sat

listening to a short, muscular farmer, Daniel Shays.

The war scar on his cheek did not damage weathered good looks, but partly contradicted an easy grin. Shays was a farmer, but the visitors sought him out now because he had been an army captain known to have seen more actual combat than most. He was known as a strong-willed leader, bold in combat.

Right now, as a farmer, he was in such sickening financial shape that he had been called to debtor's court. The visitors knew he was bitter about that, especially for the humiliation. Shays had always coveted a respectability that had not come with his birth papers. He was not a blatant social climber, but observant friends knew he yearned for dignity and the respect of his neighbors. Though he could not afford the time, he did the civic chores Pelham expected of responsible men.

He was also known to be intensely patriotic. That's why his visitors feared Shays would reject their proposal.

In the previous chapters we have seen that big government will create big debt, if allowed. To pay that debt, big government creates big taxes and big volumes of printed currency resulting in big inflation. If the inflation and rising taxes are not ultimately controlled, what would be the result in this country? We know that under foreign governments, people will tolerate drastic inflation and the resultant grueling poverty and authoritarian allocation of resources by government. But the reaction here would probably be different. One indicator is available in the Shays' record.

Shays' visitors seriously asked him to take command of a major uprising to shut down the courts of Massachusetts. They represented hundreds of desperate farmers and had been assigned to persuade Shays to accept.

In Conkey's tavern, Shays replied, "No." He was not against the idea of the uprising, but he would not lead it. He suggested the well-respected Adam Wheeler.

But Wheeler was under indictment for debts.

Shays suggested the highly regarded Job Shattuck, who had been jailed for debt.

The visitors shook their heads, "Too old."

Shays suggested fiery Luke Day, who had led forays against the debtor courts.

The visitors said Day had the taxes-and-inflation picture

mixed in with religion; he could become a fanatic dictator.

Some Pelham people in Conkey's tavern who knew what was under discussion sidled over and pressed Shays to accept.

But Shays resisted.

As you now recognize, this was happening not in the 1980s, but the 1780s.

Daniel Shays did not want to be an enemy of the country he had fought to create.

But veterans returning home from the war in 1781 stepped into a breathtaking inflation. Merchants would not accept paper dollars printed during the Revolution. They insisted on hard money—silver or gold coins. The Massachusetts government raised taxes to pay its war debts, but would not accept its own paper dollars for taxes, only hard money.

. . . the same tyranny which drove the first emigrants from home pursues their descendants still.

—Common Sense

Farmers did not earn much hard coin. And what they did earn, they needed to pay for tools from merchants who would not accept paper money. Farmers could produce their own food, but not iron tools or tax money. Therefore they became a debtor class.

A merchant creditor could easily get a judgment against a debtor farmer and seize all property except tools and clothes. If that did not satisfy the claim, he could jail the debtor. Merchants chose this course to warn other debtors.

Shays, a combat hero, had been reduced to begging credit for himself and some of his neighbors and even for the tavern keep. "Mr. Hunts: Plese to let Mr. Conkey have one quarter pound of Shugar and charg the Count to me, and you will oblige your Humbule Sarte. Daniel Shays."

In the early 1780s, Shays lived in a constant rage. In 1782, after watching a sick widow's possessions being sold for debts, he accepted appointment as Pelham's delegate to the county convention to petition the government (then called the General Court in Boston) to forbid debtor courts from prosecuting debtors until the inflation ended or until paper money became acceptable for paying all debts, including taxes.

The governor and the government refused.

That ignited the farmers statewide. In Northampton, Sam'l Ely persuaded the farmers to march on the debtor court on April 12, 1782, and "knock their grey wigs off."

As Ely's gang approached, a debtor farmer and former army captain, Luke Day, who had served seven years in the army, was arriving to be tried as a debtor. He enlisted four others and opposed Ely's mob, protecting the judges.

The court sat and jailed Ely. In June, 120 of Ely's friends marched to Springfield, Massachusetts, to shut down that court.

Meanwhile the county conventions became more active and more violent in preventing debtor courts from sitting.

The last straw was the following act by the Massachusetts lawmakers. Massachusetts had paid a lot of its Revolutionary soldiers in bounty land warrants, supposedly redeemable in western lands (100 acres for three years service). However, title to the western lands (in what is now Ohio) was not cleared. So the aging veterans, denied their lands, traded over most of these land warrants to merchants for goods at 10 cents on the dollar's worth of land.

Now the merchants, who had thus collected large bundles of these warrants, accosted the state, demanding the state pay them in dollars at the *face value of each warrant*. Since many of these merchants were also state legislators, they authorized the state to pay.

To redeem these land warrants, the state now surtaxed its citizens. Thus the impoverished veteran farmer was to be taxed so the state could pay wealthy merchants full face value for land warrants the veterans had practically given away.

It was too much.

Farmer groups assailed the courts in gangs in Northhampton, Worcester, Concord, Great Barrington, Taunton. The rebellion spread into New Hampshire and Vermont. In most cases the militia was called out to put down and arrest the farmer instigators.

The farmers needed a leader.

The committee in Conkey's tavern in Pelham, Massachusetts, pressured Shays to be that leader. Shays said he had to have time to think.

On Tuesday, September 26, 1786, Daniel Shays rode into Springfield, Massachusetts, at the head of 700 men, a fourth bearing arms. Shays' men each wore a sprig of hemlock.

Shays respectfully saluted General William Shepherd, in charge of the militia guarding the Springfield armory, and asked permission to parade. General Shepherd, seeing remnants of Continental uniforms among Shays' mob, was too shrewd to refuse.

Under the scrutiny of the militia, Shays' men paraded around the courthouse to prevent the court from sitting. The militia were identified by white paper strips attached to their clothes. Some surreptitiously stripped these off and slipped into Shays' ranks.

Shays' men prepared a petition which stated the farmers would withdraw on the judges' pledge that no debtor cases be heard without the consent of both parties, and that the farmers not be taxed for the cost of the militia arrayed against them here.

The answer from the judges came in—negative. Shays' men continued to circle the courthouse. The militia, at the order of the judges, counterparaded. Neither side wanted bloodshed.

Massachusetts Governor Bowdoin, incensed, advocated severe punishment of these rebels, and at his urging, the state senate in Boston passed a Riot Act.

Shays, still reluctantly serving as leader of the farmers driven to taking up arms against an unresponsive government, mulled over his situation. He had helped to create the very government he was now attacking. He was an enemy of his own country.

The Riot Act provided brutal punishments for armed gatherings that did not disperse within one hour after they had been read the Riot Act.

Then came January 25, 1787.

Shays and his men, who petitioned the Worcester County court "not to open" nor "to do any kind of business whatever," had been hoping the petition would be granted. However, it was denied. Shays had been offered a pardon if he submitted. He had no knowledge of either of these actions. Believing they were still in conflict, Shays prepared for major battle.

For this he needed the government cannon at Springfield.

His men arrived in Springfield about 4:00 P.M. after marching a day and a half. Although it was bitterly cold, they were in good spirits, never really expecting that General Shepherd would use the arsenal cannon against them.

Shepherd was depressed at the thought of firing on former comrades-in-arms. But Shays' rebellion now threatened to unleash a civil war. Shepherd sent an aide to beg Shays to stop and to find out what Shays wanted.

"Barracks, and the stores of the arsenal."

Shepherd warned Shays he would fire.

Shays ordered his men toward the arsenal.

When they were about 100 yards away, Shepherd ordered the cannoneers, "Fire enfilade!"

The first and second shots fell short. The third went into the ranks, as did a fourth and a fifth.

The snow turned red.

Crushed over the late-afternoon slaughter, Shays regrouped survivors and asked General Shepherd for the dead and wounded. The general replied that if Shays would only attack the arsenal again, he would be furnished with as many dead or wounded as he wished.

The militia advanced, the rebels pulled back.

Shays sent a message under a truce flag. If his men laid down arms, would everyone be pardoned and the General Court (legislature) act on the several petitions before it?

The reply came. Negative.

Instead, the governor put a price of $750 on Shays' head. The General Court declared a state of rebellion. It passed a Disqualifying Act to prevent the rebels from achieving by legislation what they were losing by insurrection. The act disqualified Shays' men from jury service, holding office, teaching school, and voting.

That act was a red flag.

Farmers in all Massachusetts towns received a circular— "Assemble your men together, see they are well armed, ready to turn out on a minute's warning, properly organized.— Shays."

Deeply saddened, Shays moved from one town to another gathering 5,000 men and spreading rebellion to other parts of New England and New York State and to the south.

We will not follow Shays' Rebellion to the end. The point

here is that it was a very major conflict nearly destroying the young nation . . . and it was caused by arrogant government creating high inflation and high taxes.

John Quincy Adams afterward said, "The Constitution was extorted from the grinding necessity of a reluctant nation. Shays' Rebellion was the extorting agency."

The noted historian Charles Francis Adams later claimed, *"Shays' Rebellion was an episode second in importance to none, one of the chief impelling and contributory causes to framing and adoption of the Constitution."*

Although the rebellion was quelled, the state leadership finally got the message. Governor Bowdoin was overwhelmingly turned out of office. A new General Court convened, with totally new members. They pardoned the rebels (except Shays), even those leaders who had been sentenced to the gallows for treason. They repealed the Disqualifying Act and outlawed imprisonment for debt.

They lowered taxes, required merchants to pay their fair share, and reduced Governor Hancock's salary. They dismissed the militia. They restored order by restoring liberty and fairness.

But we had come very close to national destruction.

Tax Rebellion Today

"Hey! There's no way something like Shays' Rebellion could happen now! Why drag up ancient history?"

FLINT TAVERN, FLINT, MICHIGAN. Like Conkey's Tavern, the Flint is, besides a place for strong waters, an exchange for strong thoughts today.

Here and in other forums in southeast Michigan, from Flint to Detroit, the strong thoughts are leading the debaters to join several organizations, including one called We the People, founded by Dean Hazel, an infuriated hourly worker at a GM plant in Pontiac. The organization operates from a storefront in Pontiac. Its purpose, along with that of other organizations, is to oppose outrageous taxation.

These are not merely talking groups making idle noise.

This is a taxpayer rebellion like Shays'. Thousands of outraged citizens are either refusing to file income tax returns or are claiming ninety-nine dependents each so that no income tax is withheld.

Leonard Nawrocki, an IRS manager of criminal investigation, estimated 3,500 workers in Michigan are changing filing status or not filing in one recent year. The numbers are growing, "That's the secret—the numbers. I don't think we can prosecute them all."

Dean Hazel said We the People "are not income tax evaders or cheats. If Nawrocki wants to haul our guys into court, he'll get his ears pinned back."

The IRS is stepping up audits and warning protestors they could go to jail. But the numbers are growing.

Shades of Shays.

One might say, "That's an intellectual rebellion; Americans would never again stage a large physical violence type rebellion."

Do you remember the Watts uprising in California? Watts Avenue finally stretched out across the nation to Woodward Avenue in Detroit, Hough Avenue in Cleveland, and then to Dayton, Newark, Rochester, and other cities.

But Michigan is only one small part of the United States. Even if you throw in California's Proposition 13 and Massachusetts' Proposition 2½, it is not a national rebellion.

Isn't it?

Much of the national tax rebellion is invisible but all-pervasive. A painting contractor in Westlake, Ohio, brought back his bid quotation in person, verbally not in writing. "For doing all the basement woodwork, patching the living room ceiling and the kitchen ceiling, it will be $975."

The customer knew all costs were up. Still that total surprised him. "I'll need a couple days to consider whether I can afford it."

"Sure."

The contractor turned as if to leave, but he paused in the open doorway. "However...I have a suggestion for lowering that quote 25 percent if you're interested."

"Of course I'm interested."

"Would you be willing to pay me half by check and half in cash?"

The subterranean cash tax-free economy in the United States today is estimated by nearly all business journals as roaring along at an overwhelming $200 billion.

At first that seems improbable, because our major industries obviously operate by checks.

However, consider the potential daily cash transactions by millions of individuals in thousands of cities and towns in our 3000 counties. Then $200 billion per year in subterranean cash transaction is no surprise.

This is a national rebellion against giantism in taxation and against its invisible tax collector, government-spawned inflation.

The Potential for Upheaval

The mood for rebellion exists.

We have seen it developing. As people despair of getting government action via normal democratic processes, they switch to mass protests, sit-ins, tractor convoys, Watts-type riots.

We in no way sympathize with destructive riots; we only point out that the ice has been broken for rebellion in modern times. It can happen here.

Other observers agree. Have you noticed the whole school of unlovely books by nevertheless shrewd authors, counseling survivalists in matter-of-fact tones?

- *How to Survive the Upcoming Financial Disaster*
- *How Can You Protect Yourself?*
- *What to Do When the Financial Chaos Comes*
- *Inflation and Liberty*

Those are just a few examples. They advise buying homes way out in the country to avoid rebellious mobs, hoarding canned goods, buying gold, possessing firearms for protection.

"That's a bunch of baloney. That stuff can't happen here."

One would like to think not.

And yet...most lifelong students of inflation come to the same conclusion as Hans F. Sennholz in his *Age of Inflation.*

How will the American people take to depression (born of inflation) and deterioration? The reaction may be militant and violent. Guided by doctrines of conflict and convinced of their inalienable rights to government care and egalitarian redistribution, they may insist on their rights. After all, our transfer politicians, parties, and intellectuals have for forty years convinced them of the social justice of their claims. Are these now to be abrogated in the face of economic adversity? Moreover, their collective organizations wield the necessary political power to extract their due share from the body politic. But if this body should fail to yield the expected benefits, will the millions of beneficiaries peacefully suffer the welfare cuts? If they do not, our redistributive society may be torn asunder by civil conflict and strife. Business establishments may be looted, our cities burned, and law and order may give way to violent disorder. Since the first redistributive measure, several decades ago, this has been the ultimate destination of the Redistributive State.

That doesn't seem possible.

And yet, by degrees, without noticing the escalation, we are routinely accepting direct action forms of political expression by those wishing to force action: sit-ins, rallies, marches, wildcat strikes, people refusing to pay taxes.

Sennholz forecasts:

Finally, economic and social deterioration of such major magnitude strengthens the call for law and order. When society can no longer cooperate voluntarily and peacefully, the raw power of the State will be used. Vast emergency power will be thrust on the President, who will be expected to restore civil order. For this grim task, the most ruthless politician is likely to rise to the top. They'll bring the peace that is totally inimical to individual enterprise and personal freedom.

Isn't that the same climate that ignited Shays' Rebellion?

Common-Sense Taxation

This book favors taxes.

But there are honest taxes and pickpocket taxes. Government inflationary printing of money is a hidden pickpocket tax.

All taxes must be visible.

That requires balancing the budget. To do that we must cut expenses so that tax revenue covers expenses without borrowing. Visible taxes might even have to be *raised* temporarily to cover expenses until the cost of government is reduced. Even that raise would be acceptable if it was en route to balancing the budget and ultimately lowering taxes and reducing the invisible inflation tax.

It is common sense that income tax reports, both regular and negative income tax reports, should be simple, easy to understand, and easy to prepare. Can you imagine the recklessness of basing the nation's very income on forms and formulas so complex that even its most sophisticated citizens find them difficult to comprehend and IRS personnel themselves interpret them differently?

The negative income tax could start at near the necessity cost of living for those without income, decreasing to zero when the income level rises to that necessity cost of living.

And it would seem common sense for regular income tax to start low in relation to the necessity cost of living. Income tax rates would then increase with income to a modest maximum, say 30 percent.

Very few deductions should be permitted. The 20/20 deductions for personal saving and for charitable giving, plus interest on home mortgages, would seem sufficient. This should permit a low income tax rate range. So-called tax loopholes and shelters ought to be avoided.

While this would put battalions of creative tax consultants out of work, it would probably increase revenue. Reducing maximum income tax reduces the incentive for tax evasion.

Any additional other personal taxes, such as noncharitable gift and estate taxes, should be in reasonable relationship to the income tax range. Further taxes, if necessary, should be visible consumption taxes (except for necessity foods).

A balanced budget is basic. If the national debt increases when times are bad, then it should be reduced when times are good so the national debt is controlled and maintains a relationship to the real value of the national economy.

In balancing the budget, there are still other sources of government revenue.

As owner of nearly a fourth of our land mass, government can sell certain government lands for development of natural resources. When direct sale is undesirable, it may lease lands temporarily.

Additionally, services that government now renders free to small segments of the population can be billed directly to the users. That is common sense. Our consular services, for example, are utilized by a minority of our citizens and businesses. Why should Joe Pinga's bakery be paying part of the costs of American consuls around the world? He sells no pastry abroad. Let those who use specialized services pay for them. Not Joe. It's common sense.

And by a plain method of argument, as we are running the next generation into debt, we ought to do the work of it; otherwise we use them. . . pitifully. In order to discover the line of our duty rightly, we should take our children in our hand and fix our station a few years farther into life; that eminence will present a prospect which a few present years and prejudices conceal from our sight.

—Common Sense

The action of Dean Hazel of Flint, Michigan, and Daniel Shays of Pelham, Massachusetts, are separated by 190 years; but they give the same warning: The common man demands a government run by common sense.

Unfortunately, today's government appears determined to illustrate an observation made by Ralph Waldo Emerson: "Nothing astonishes men so much as common sense and plain dealing." The American public, however, is more than ready for the surprise.

7

MORE FREEDOM

A Highly Personal Matter

Democratic Strength

Tom Paine warned that *government must remain personal* even though it will be difficult to *keep* it personal. If it ceases being personal, freedom will cease.

> *In the first parliament every man by natural right will have a seat.*
> *But as the colony increases... and the distance at which members may be separated... too inconvenient for all of them to meet on every occasion as at first....*
> —Common Sense

Democratic strength depends upon the individual.

The point is made here because the citizenry now believes the national condition has outgrown the citizen's personal ability to handle it. We have delegated the handling of it to men who said they knew what to do. They didn't.

The collective common sense of *personally involved citizens is sounder than the supposed expertise of government specialists. This is important to remember, because we are coming to three big jobs that citizens will try to duck on the grounds that they are too big for individuals to take on.*

The Three Big Ones

To replace a blown fuse in your 110-volt line in the dark, have you ever first had to repair your 1-1/2 volt flashlight?

To correct big government, big welfare, big inflation, and big taxation, there are some flashlights and small tools we need to repair first to shed light or provide leverage on the big fix. These are:

- *Education,* on which depends the whole ability of citizens to operate a large democracy.
- *Security,* which is the chief function of government.
- *Good will toward each other,* which is the chief deterrent to big government.

You think those subjects are too big for you to handle, but it is exactly *because* they are so big that you must handle them personally, not delegate them to your government. You may assign them to your government for action, but *you must retain the policymaking role* of the sovereign citizen.

Do we have naive confidence in the judgment of the common man?

No. The public can be an idiot—cruel, selfish, and misguided.

The massed public can be duped or coerced into looking away from an Auschwitz or a Watergate, but they usually don't *start* them. Governments do. The public, with all its callous ignorance, if it remains free, finally seems to come down on the side of common sense. We have seen it recently dump two American presidents, forcing one to resign, embarrassing the other with a cold shoulder at the polls.

Certain sound conclusions are within the province of men and women of common sense in bridge clubs, barber shops, or in Flint and Conkeys' Taverns, U.S.A.

You may challenge, "The public didn't discover the big faults; the media did it." True, but free press is part of the public.

Education: The Fourth Necessity of Life

If we are to retain freedom in a complex world, we must recognize a fourth necessity of life in America—education. You can no longer afford a dummy for a neighbor.

It is on the sound education of the people that the security and destiny of every nation chiefly exists.

—Louis Kossuth.

Additionally, you need the all-powerful benefit of your neighbor's creative initiative, sharpened by education. Therein lies the great buoyant power of democratic strength.

Education is a complex project conducted by an enormous cadre of trained professionals. And we do not intend to intrude into that professional turf, only into one common-sense aspect, the delivery system.

Our point is not that educators today are doing too little, but that they are attempting too much. Our schools are still trying to give full service to the largest group of customers served by any industry. *Every* other mass consumer industry has rolled the workload back onto the customer.

The education customer, however, still expects to drive in, plug in, have education pumped into the tank, and drive out. While the teacher scurries around to all the hoses trying to pump all this education and check the oil and tires, the student sits relaxed, a spectator to his own education.

Industry long ago discovered the solution to mass consumer service. Time was—the grocer would discuss the ham with you, cut it, weigh it, wrap it, even deliver it. No more. The high labor cost era overwhelmed that. The self-service supermarket came. Read your own labels, select your own groceries, carry them out to your car yourself. The customer does the work.

The telephone company followed swiftly. Dial your own long distance.

The banks. Make your own deposits, withdrawals, even loans in the electronic teller. The customer does the work.

Mass feeding cafeterias have always used the self-service idea; but today even the deluxe restaurant tells you to make your own salad, then serve yourself at the buffet.

As labor costs catch up with each industry, it puts the work back on the customer. Even at the so-called service station, now you pump your gasoline.

In numbers of customers, all of these industries are smaller than the education industry.

How long can education, the most expensive per capita product the average mass consumer buys, resist the solution found necessary by all other mass consumer industries? Typical education costs per student per year in the suburbs of Cleveland range from $1,374 in Strongsville to $4,282 in Cleveland Heights, and rising.

We propose solo learning. Retain the school building, the classroom, and the teacher. But have the student come in *to teach himself* under the guidance of the teacher.

Far fetched?

It already happens. In graduate school, the professor tells students at the outset what they are expected to learn. He gives them a few tips about where to find it and how to learn it. Then they hardly see him again until he shows up to give them the test.

Move down a notch. College honors courses use the same method.

The merit of this goes far beyond economics. Much more important than learning facts like the effect of molybdenum and tungsten on the tensile strength of steel alloys, the students learn how to learn.

Increasingly in this era of rapid technological change a person may have to stop in midlife to teach himself a new vocation as progress makes certain trades and professions obsolete.

Still more important, the citizen needs to be able to inform him*self* of national problems so that he can direct his government with common sense.

Moving the solo-learning concept gradually down to the high school and then to elementary grades could create a nation of powerful, effective citizens who possess the key to wherever they want to to go in life—the ability to teach themselves and the ability to supervise their governments.

Can you imagine the power of that!

Solo learning frees the teacher to work individually with each student who hits a snag. It frees the gifted child from lockstep to the medium, lets him assist the teacher with the whole class. Kids learn well from kids.

Now the student is no longer a bored spectator on the fifty-yard line of his own education. He is out on the field in the game. When he completes a self-taught education, he has become a powerful human being, owning the highest skill available—*the ability to develop himself.*

A nation of citizens who can teach themselves can take back

its government into its own hands. It will know when someone is running away with the powers reserved to the people. It can better evaluate candidates.

The self-education technique is well within the state of the art and capability of educators today. It can be implemented with or without computer assistance. Of course, nowadays even the primary school tots are friends with the computer. As R.A.W. Rudd told an international gathering of bankers, "Because of the extraordinary speed of innovation which the microchip is opening up...the whole of our economic and social lives will shortly be permeated by the revolutionary effects of this new wave of technology."

Most important, solo learning can make quality education affordable. The present system will send costs off the charts, beyond our reach.

And education does need improvement. The public school monopoly would be stimulated by the competition of strong, aggressive private schools. Private schools need encouragement by some tax consideration to families sending their children to nonpublic schools.

Security

The citizen's daily paper constantly briefs him on the barrage of threats to security, internal and external. No elaboration is needed here.

But what of solutions?

A major part of defense is the conduct of our foreign relations, in which one significant change is indicated to men of common sense. It has a place in this book because it will lead to preserving the sound dollar, preserving a strong economy, and therefore preserving liberty.

June 12, 1980. Letter to the Editor, Cleveland Press:
Dear Editor:
One day a very kind American walked down to the lake. He saw a hungry alligator swimming in the water. I must feed the alligator, he said, and he went and sought a large piece of meat.

The next day there were two alligators and the man had to get his neighbors to help him buy meat.

Soon there were many people feeding many alligators. Surprisingly, the alligators did not seem to appreciate the food and would bite the arms and legs off the people feeding them. The people only blamed themselves for not buying more meat.

This is the story of foreign aid, and there are still those who wonder why so many people hate Americans

C. *CALVIN WRIGHT,* 1496 Lakwood Ave.,
Lakewood, Ohio

It behooves the citizen now to look straight on at the dislike, even hatred, which has been bought for us at staggering, little-known cost to us.

Foreign relations are similar to personal relations. In a common-sense way we know in our hearts that if you put a good man in your debt with gifts that make him dependent, you diminish his self-respect and competence and independence. For that, even as he says, "Muchas gracias," he will never forgive you.

The answer is trade, not aid.

The Agency for International Development, U.S. State Department, lists the tragic record. Much of the following money we borrowed to give away in a twenty-eight-year period to 147 nations, charging the U.S. taxpayer for principal and interest.

Afghanistan $463,900,000
Bangladesh 525,600,000
Cyprus 29,500,000
Egypt 891,600,000
Greece 4,253,300,000
India 9,026,400,000
Iran 2,129,100,000
Iraq 93,300,000
Israel 5,204,500,000
Jordan 1,084,200,000
Lebanon 151,000,000
Nepal 198,600,000
Pakistan 4,982,400,000
Saudi Arabia 326,500,000
Sri Lanka 214,300,000
Syria 61,200,000
Turkey 6,608,600,000

Yemen, People's Democratic
  Republic of 4,500,000
Yemen Arab Republic 50,000,000
Central Treaty Organization 52,700,000
Near East and South
  Asia Regional 459,000,0000

Argentina..................................394,800,000
Bahamas 300,000
Barbados 1,200,000
Belize 6,900,000
Bolivia 663,900,000
Brazil...................................2,913,800,000
Chile...................................1,125,800,000
Colombia 1,424,700,000
Costa Rica................................199,800,000
Cuba..16,400,000
Dominican Republic........................520,800,000
Ecuador 345,600,000
El Salvador 162,500,000
Guatemala 329,400,000
Guyana......................................80,400,000
Haiti.....................................121,300,000
Honduras..................................169,700,000
Jamaica 99,800,000
Mexico....................................297,900,000
Nicaragua.................................223,700,000
Panama 317,000,000
Paraguay 167,500,000
Peru 598,000,000
Surinam 5,800,000
Trinidad and Tobago........................40,500,000
Uruguay...................................210,300,000
Venezuela.................................340,300,000
Other West Indies..........................13,000,000
ROCAP 247,800,000
East Caribbean Regional 33,000,000
Latin America Regional 3,192,400,000

Burma.....................................185,000,000

Cambodia.................................1,799,400,000
China, Republic of 5,708,500,000
Hong Kong 43,800,000
Indochina, Undistributed 1,542,500,000
Indonesia 1,991,500,000
Japan....................................3,834,100,000
Korea 11,360,500,000
Laos.....................................2,521,700,000
Malaysia.................................131,000,000
Philippines 2,355,600,000
Ryukyu Islands 413,700,000
Singapore.................................23,500,000
Thailand.................................1,898,600,000
Vietnam 22,356,300,000
Western Samoa 4,000,000
East Asia Regional 422,700,000

Algeria 180,400,000
Bolswana 33,900,000
Burundi 10,300,000
Cameroon 34,400,000
Central African Republic.....................6,800,000
Chad.....................................17,900,000
Congo,Peoples Republic of the 5,600,000
Dahomey 15,600,000
Ethiopia 538,400,000
Gabon....................................7,800,000
The Gambia 7,100,000
Ghana....................................283,300,000
Guinea 105,900,000
Ivory Coast 35,900,000
Kenya....................................112,000,000
Lesotho...................................19,000,000
Liberia 229,700,000
Libya 228,600,000
Malagasy Republic..........................15,900,000
Malawi...................................30,700,000
Mali, Republic of 52,400,000
Mauritania................................16,400,000
Mauritius.................................12,900,000

Morocco.....................................938,800,000
Niger 47,200,000
Nigeria....................................410,100,000
Rwanda 8,800,000
Senegal.....................................52,000,000
Seychelles......................................500,000
Sierra Leone 44,800,000
Somali Republic 77,100,000
South Africa, Republic of 1,300,000
Southern Rhodesia 7,000,000
Sudan.....................................120,600,000
Swaziland..................................7,700,000
Tanzania....................................94,800,000
Togo 22,900,000
Tunisia 799,500,000
Uganda......................................42,900,000
Upper Volta................................34,100,000
Zaire.....................................501,900,000
Zambia.....................................33,800,000
Central and West Africa
    Regional...............................115,700,0000
East Africa Regional........................34,300,000
Southern Africa Regional....................56,400,000
Africa Regional............................246,000,000

Albania...................................20,400,000
Austria 1,251,200,000
Belgium-Luxembourg 1,853,100,000
Czechoslovakia 193,000,000
Denmark 907,800,000
Finland....................................56,900,000
France...................................8,273,500,000
German Democratic Republic 800,000
Germany (Federal Republic) 4,979,300,000
Berlin 131,900,000
Hungary....................................32,700,000
Iceland 82,000,000
Ireland 146,500,000
Italy.....................................5,688,800.000
Malta 43,200,000
Netherlands 2,282,800,000

Norway 1,216,200,0000
Poland 539,300,000
Portugal 505,700,000
Romania. 9,700,000
Spain 1,882,800,000
Sweden 109,000,000
United Kingdom 8,730,800,000
U.S.S.R. 186,400,000
Yugoslavia. 2,747,400,000
Europe Regional 835,800,000

Australia. 123,600,000
New Zealand 8,600,000
Papua New Guinea 300,000
Trust Territory of the
    Pacific Islands 528,600,000
Other Oceania. 9,800,000
Canada. 30,600,000
Interregional. 15,334,500,000
Grand Total $172,109,000,000*

*The figures here, supplied by the Agency for International Develop-
ment, show the giveaway record up to 1975 only. Seventeen of the indicated amounts were in the form of loans rather than outright
grants. However, as of 1975, only some $3.6 billion had been repaid
in full with interest. While in the intervening years accounts have
been put in order with a number of countries owing money on loans,
the amount is relatively insignificant compared to further billions
given away or no longer recoverable as loans. And all this is taxpayers' money. (Chart reprinted from *What Has Really Changed?*, a publication of the Warner & Swasey Company, p. 74-1975.)

We've institutionalized welfare. To weaken ourselves by
draining off that much of our substance could be worth it if we
had strengthened the rest of the world by that much, whether or
not they became our friends. But an American can scan his
daily paper from front to back for a year and find no paragraph
of documentation that the massive program has accomplished
anything for the peoples of the world or for himself.

He can read of damage it has caused. He can read of dependency it has caused. He can read of misdirection of funds to fac-
tions that are our professed enemies. One has the vision of a

giant bleeding U.S. buffalo surrounded by laughing wolves. History may call our handling of foreign aid a gigantic naivete.

Foreign aid programs of the past few decades have no similarity to the Marshall Plan, which provided dramatic results shortly after World War II. Additionally, the Marshall Plan legislative leaders were aware they were about to give away huge chunks of America ($17 billion planned, $12.5 billion actual) and that therefore they should *consult* Americans. So they launched a massive three-month selling campaign to the grass roots, amounting nearly to a national referendum. The American people said, yes. Only then did Congress pass the Marshall Plan. Today, however, the great giveaway is quietly institutionalized, the public totally unaware of the recipients or the amounts or purposes.

Are we proposing to cut all foreign aid? Certainly not. But we should start over with a clean sheet of paper, deep knowledge of what we are doing, and firm intent to deinstitutionalize international welfare. To qualify for aid, nations should prove results achieved with funds already received.

For the most part, common-sense aid would take the form of technical know-how transfer to help nations help themselves develop industrially and commercially, followed by trading with those nations on a commercial basis. For example, unlimited solar energy may be the power of the future, and technical assistance there could fuel many third-world countries into economic leadership.

Our actions prompting self-reliance will demonstrate to nations better than gifts the cause and effect relationship between freedom and a good personal and national life. They will experience democratic strength rather than read about it on the unconvincing propaganda wrapper around a foreign aid gift.

But what of our traditional concern for human rights around the world? Should we abandon the attempt to promote human rights?

No!

But we have proved expensively that we cannot buy human rights with gifts. We have proved we cannot really identify which faction within another nation truly champions human rights.

How then do we operate among nations without abandoning our dedication to human rights?

There is growing consensus that until some as yet uninvented super technique arrives, our strongest method of spreading human rights around the world is to sustain the world's best example here. To many in the world, for two hundred years America has been less a piece of geography than an idea, a dream. People have begged, borrowed, and stolen across waters at night to get here. They still do. They come for the freedom, and incidentally they found freedom to have a great side benefit. They wrote home the surprising news that individual freedom in some mysterious way unleashes creative initiative, inventiveness, and imagination so that it also produces the better life. Individual freedom and prosperity are strangely related. That is democratic strength.

As former President Carter correctly explained, "The great democracies are not free because they are rich. They are rich because they are free."

After Thomas Paine's slim volume did its work here, the book and the idea traveled on around the world, and as new nations emerge, it is still studied. Some say the book is on its fifth trip around the world.

Active interference by the United States in the internal affairs of foreign nations produces more problems than solutions. Our best role is to be the example. To do that well we must get our own house in order...again. If we do a superb job of that, releasing the creative initiative of millions here, the tyrannical state concept should fall of its own weight in glaring contrast.

The communist economies, according to Hans F. Sennholz in the *Freeman*, May 1981, are straining to achieve production of minimum life necessities, with no hope of providing the working man the life available in free countries.

One reason the contrast may be less visible is because of a strange move on the part of Western nations. Since 1970, Western governments and financial institutions have loaned the Soviet bloc at least $88 billion. Why? It is our traditional multi-billion-dollar bungle: building up with the left hand what we oppose with the right.

The World Bank, heavily supported by American taxpayers, is bound up in the same bungle.

How many nation-states are there in the world?

Guess high.

The National Intelligence Factbook compiled by the CIA describes, from Abu Dhabi to Zambia, 187 nations. They are in various stages of development and sophistication, speaking over one hundred languages.

We cannot very long financially support 147 of these 187 nations with gifts and loans. Our best chance is to assist them to help themselves become self-sufficient, so they become world contributors and strong allies.

What is the merit of bankrupting ourselves, pouring huge monies into other nations, allowing them to reduce their own taxes at the expense of our taxpayers?

This is common sense?

Many feel our best chance and our best policy is to treat all foreign nations with even-handed respect—avoid commercial agreements that show partiality and let free competition operate largely minus duties and quotas. Yet, realistically, to maintain trade balance and protect against unfair trade practices, it may become necessary at times to impose tariffs. If so, use common sense. Keep them simple with a flat percentage across the board by nation or trading area, determined by straightforward calculations that cannot be influenced by special interests.

Sometimes free competition will hurt some of our own industries temporarily. But the long-term result of free competition is to create sound operations based on realism. Protectionism is daydreaming; it supports artificially high wages and only temporarily. Our citizens pay for this deception in artificially high prices.

Defense

Defense is the principal role of government.

We have big enemies. Hostile nations and internal organized crime. Our government is responsible to us for defense against both.

We will not intrude into the technology of police work or military weaponry. But as we see it, good internal and external security, as best practiced, get down to the common-sense philosophy practiced aboard the tanker *Sable Bay*.

While millions of words are written about defense, most men and most kids instinctively know the ancient common-sense truth reenacted for the multimillionth time on this rusting U.S. merchant ship.

The whole story was reported by George Morrill, a powerful reporter of the sea. He witnessed it as a seaman on the battered U.S. merchant tanker *Sable Bay*.

Off an Italian port, a young sailor with shoulders like spars was choppered aboard from the replacement pool. He dropped a lumpy seabag on deck and carefully placed beside it a portable typewriter. "My name is Bud Harkness," he smiled pleasantly.

Morrill, affected by the particularly vicious environment on the *Sable Bay*, growled, "If you want to get along on this tub, better deep six the girlie machine."

In twenty-four hours, young Harkness discovered that meanness was the way of life on the *Sable Bay*. Razor, a fireman, poured scalding coffee down the mess boy's shirt. Frenchy slung a plate of beans at the cook. A drunken mate threw a sailor off the fantail into the sea.

The night the ship sailed for Suez, Harkness asked Morrill, "What's wrong on this tub?"

Morrill explained. The character of the captain and the executive officer fostered violence, favoritism, injustice, and intramural wars.

One day, while Harkness was off watch, drinking a can of orange juice and working at his typewriter on the fantail, a big puffy-eyed seamen named Jim Tracy came up and watched in sneering silence. A half dozen seamen lounged around. Finally Tracy walked over and lowered a large hand flat onto the keyboard, jamming it. "Did I do something?" He grinned maliciously.

Harkness didn't answer. He opened some new cans of juice and handed them around, including Tracy. Bud chugalugged his, then he held the can lengthwise between his thumb and forefinger, getting Tracy's attention. He slowly squeezed, crunching the can.

Then he untangled the typewriter. "Got to take it easy on these machines, Jim. Okay?"

Jim Tracy backed off with a sheepish smile.

One day Frenchy, a mustachioed giant and a confessed former boxer, brazenly ate a deckhand's whole can of peanuts. Bud confronted Frenchy with the empty can. "Sure I ate 'em. Why not?"

Bud dropped to the deck and did five fast one-armed push-ups. He came off the deck and made a few playful boxing moves close by Frenchy's chin, but jackhammer fast.

Frenchy turned up his palms, "Look, I'll get the guy some peanuts at Abadan."

Gradually a few of the crew began hanging out with Bud. They began working out with him with the weights and jump ropes. They ate with him in the mess. They became known as "the outfit." Whenever some trouble was brewing aboard, the outfit would merely walk up to the trouble and just stand there, staring. Trouble walked away.

One night a steward came running up to the outfit on the fantail, "Trouble in the mess."

Bud took off, the outfit following. In the mess, a third engineer and three oilers had the cook and the mess boys with their arms behind their backs to force them to open the freezer. The engineer threatened them with a whiplike whirling rope.

The outfit started to charge the oilers, but Harkness spread his arms as a barrier. He lifted down the strap-like steel bar on which the pans hung. He took a deep breath and slowly bent the bar into a U, then hung it over one oiler's shoulder. The oilers stared at the bar, then slowly released the mess boys and eased themselves out.

The outfit started after them. Harkness blocked them.

"Why not?" challenged one of his new friends.

"The job is done," Harkness said. *"Put solid force on display; you don't have to use it."*

That would be an ideal U.S. national defense policy—internal and external—a strong military force, backed by a strong economy, backed up by a strong citizenry.

Democratic strength, with its release of the creative initiative of millions of people, is the best foundation for military strength. Advances in technology such as the microchip, photo reconnaissance, and digital radar systems can reduce the military manpower needed and improve effectiveness. It can reduce the need for nuclear weapons, reduce unnecessary damage inflicted on the enemy and provide more effective defense.

Further, continually developing defensive and offensive military equipment that makes existing weaponry obsolete is the best national defense, also reducing the cost of it.

In World War II, France's old expensive Maginot Line did not keep Hitler's *Blitzkrieg* from overrunning France. However,

Britain's Royal Air Force with its new Spitfire fighter planes kept the German Luftwaffe from winning the Battle of Britain.

It is common knowledge at this writing that the Soviets have total contempt for those who deal from weakness.

Henry Kissinger has stated that the survival of America and the world depends on a couple of fundamentals:

- restoration of United States military parity;
- formulation of a consistent U.S. foreign policy that makes it clearly advantageous for someone to be our friend and disadvantageous to be our adversary.

Kissinger, a realist, sees the United States frittering away our advantages.

People do not like to hear that, pretend not to hear it. That is dangerous. The tragic failure to recognize the danger of Hitler tore up the world and killed more than 20 million people.

Our strength and our policy must be clear to our friends and to our opponents. That includes internal enemies: organized crime, unorganized crime and corruption in very high places. These enemies also need to see convincing strength of defense.

Then the citizens must control the defense to see that it does not itself become our enemy.

The Most Secret Equation

We have discovered many of nature's powerfully balanced equations, giving rise to our advanced technologies. For example, every action has an equal and opposite reaction; we've applied that principle to build machines. Energy conversion: Input equals output in different form. Matter conversion: Input equals output by weight.

Nature's balanced equations continue on into the animal partnerships. The Zick Zack plover lives in symbiotic relationship with the crocodile. The Zick Zack feeds by eating leeches off the crocodile's back and by picking the teeth of the croc. The crocodile in turn is warned of danger by the piercing cry of the perceptive Zick Zack perched as sentinel high in the trees.

The oak tree feeds and houses the squirrel. The squirrel propagates the oaks, spreading and burying acorns.

Small horse mackerel swim under the protective umbrellas of

giant jelly fish. The pilot fish everlastingly accompanies his partner, the shark. Beefeater birds clean the hides of cattle. Sea anemones attach themselves to the hermit crab and trade favors for food.

These are not exceptions. No animal lives or dies for itself.

Man and animal also lived that balanced equation for centuries. The drayman took good care of his giant Belgian horses. The horses furnished the drayman a living.

All these equations we mastered well, but not the next step— one man's relationship to another, how we take care of the other guy. This is a highly personal matter. The balanced equation is still there in the long run, but we haven't examined or applied it with conviction. We have not proved it to our satisfaction, as we have in chemistry, physics, biology, botany, and zoology—that if we take good care of the other guy, he takes care of us.

In that ignorance lies the gaping opening for the growth of giant government. The better we treat the other guy, the less government we need, the less taxes we pay, the less inflation we spawn, the more freedom we preserve.

Tom Paine saw the hidden but absolute relationship between freedom and treating the other fellow right.

Some writers have so confounded society with government as to leave little or no distinction between them, whereas they are not only different but have different origins. Society is produced by our wants, and government by our wickedness; the former promotes our happiness positively by uniting our affections, the latter negatively by restraining our vices. The one encourages intercourse, the other creates distinctions. The first is a patron, the last a punisher. . . .

In order to gain a clear and just idea of the design and end of government, let us suppose a small number of persons settled in some sequestered part of the earth, unconnected with the rest; they will then represent the first peopling of any country, or of the world. In this state of natural liberty, society will be their first thought. A thousand motives will excite them thereto; the strength of one man is so unequal to his wants and his mind so unfitted for perpetual solitude that he is soon obliged to seek assistance and relief of another, who in his turn requires the same. Four or five united would be able to raise a tolerable dwelling in the midst of a wilderness, but one man might labor out the common period of life without accomplishing anything; when he had felled his timber, he could not remove it, nor erect it after it was removed; hunger in the meantime would urge him from his work and every different want call him a different way. Disease, nay even misfortune, would be death; for though neither might be mortal, yet either would disable him from living and reduce him to a state in which he might rather be said to perish than to die.

Thus necessity, like a gravitating power, would soon form our newly arrived emigrants into society, the reciprocal blessing of which would supersede and render the obligations of law and government unnecessary while they remained perfectly just to each other; but as nothing but Heaven is impregnable to vice, it will unavoidably happen that in proportion as they surmount the first difficulties of emigration, which bound them together in a common cause, they will begin to relax in their duty and attachment to each other, and this remissness will point out the necessity of establishing some form of government to supply the defect of moral virtue.

—Common Sense

As we increase the quality of our personal treatment of the other guy, we decrease the need for government.

It is a very personal matter.

It is between you and me.

8

MORE VOTER ACTION

Freedom Via the Dollar

Freedom.

Over half the world is trying to get it.

We had it, and we are dumping it.

We are seeing, as in Shays' Rebellion and under current conditions, that freedom depends on sound money. The linkage is as imperious as a law of nature. When we can provide our own daily bread, we are free. Otherwise no. In the 1960s young Americans instinctively and correctly nicknamed money—*bread*.

When, via inflation, we lose the ability to obtain our own bread, the government that has made us dependent by inflation then requires nearly dictatorial powers to feed us. It must take from you to feed me—and then some.

The direct route back to liberty is to *reverse the shrinkage of that dollar* to regain the ability to obtain our own bread, with plenty left over to take care of the handicapped.

In the face of all the large organizations pressuring politicians

SUPPORT YOUR LOCAL SDCAC

for inflationary programs, where does one individual get any clout? Through the recently invented device of *the political action committee*. Any group of citizens can organize themselves into a PAC to supply election campaign funds to the candidates of their choice. Some PACs organize around broad political philosophies, others around narrow single issues.

We propose. . . . right now. . . . that citizens organize, locally and nationally, to form sound-dollar citizen action committees—SDCACs. Attorneys and legislators can explain the steps for organizing.

The SDCAC would concentrate exclusively on the return to a sound dollar, channeling campaign funds pointedly to candidates committed to legislating for that. The committee would monitor the legislative records of political figures and report voting records of each to the membership. The SDCAC would target its funds to elect specific candidates and to defeat others.

This single move automatically implements many other roads back to freedom, because the SDCACs would come down on the side of:

- reduction of governments, with substitution of private contractors;
- taxation laws that encourage personal saving, investment, and employment;
- limitation of government spending to a fixed share of national income;
- abolishing regulations that cost more than the benefits returned;
- reduction of world trade barriers;
- taxation that encourages private giving and concern for the other guy; a generous incentive to take care of each other.

The CAC gains strength through assembling a large enough kitty of votes to command candidate respect. It cannot be patted on the head and then brushed off. In addition, the money comes from a large number of small contributors, avoiding the hazard of influence-buying.

The fatal enemy of democracy is a sleeping citizenry. The SDCAC would not sleep. SDCACs would monitor progress in reducing taxes and thereby getting the load off the taxpayer's back. They would periodically report to members the changing buying power of the dollar.

The SDCAC organization can thus do a very thorough job that the individual citizen cannot, scanning all legislation in progress in the legislatures within its area. It can then do a thorough survey of the intentions of candidates toward legislation. This would be a full-time job beyond the capacity of the individual citizen. But each citizen can contribute five dollars or more to the SDCAC to accomplish this.

And in so doing, the citizen can again become, as he was before we threw away our sovereign rights, the boss.

In the real world, where strong special interests organize into power blocs to gain extra representation with legislators, overriding the apathetic individual citizen's influence, the unaffiliated citizen needs equal representational clout to defeat inflation, the natural enemy of democracies, which do not usually have a history of long life. If this democracy is to continue, which is already a serious worry, a sound-dollar political action committee's monitoring should be continuous over the decades much like the action of the admirable League of Women Voters.

The natural tendency is for all governments to prefer inflation to honest direct taxation. The SDCAC is a must to prevent worthless currency.

Turn Pro

What else can we do?

Let us not be naive. No bunch of born-again patriots is going to march out and grab our government back via high-school civics techniques steamed up with righteous indignation. The professionals in our capital will stiff-arm us with bland grins, then run over us like the Oakland Raiders playing the local high school junior varsity team. We won't even see the ball the first two seasons.

As a long and violent abuse of power is generally the means of calling the right of it in question.

—Common Sense

The common sense of it is that to take your government back into your own hands from professionals, *you must become a professional citizen.*

Why you?

First, because legally, you are the government. Nobody remembers that. You will need to remind everybody. They will laugh at first, even the judges. For example, Cleveland at this writing has a federal judge usurping the function of the people's elected school board.

Second, you are the only one who can take the government back for you. The previous generation cannot. They gave it away. Most retreated into their private lives, abdicating. Some retreated into single-issue special interest constituencies, crowding out the general citizen, who became unrepresented.

So it must be you.

Probably you, too, will abdicate.

Apathy—yours and ours—is the enemy.

I mean not to exhibit horror for the purpose of provoking revenge, but to awaken us from fatal and unmanly slumbers.

—Common Sense

But in case you decide not to abdicate, here is the action.

Take a time pledge. Use common sense. The pros you're going up against invest the time. They even work nights at the politics of it. There is no way we are going to take our government back into our own hands without putting in some time. But do not commit too much time, or before long you will abandon the whole effort.

The present winter is worth an age if rightly employed, but if lost or neglected the whole continent will partake of the misfortune.

—Common Sense

Give an hour a week for the U.S.A. One hour per week by each of us would be revolutionary and reclaim our democracy. Isn't that worth as much time as bowling?

What can we do with that hour per week?

Think Small (At First)

Did you start at the top at school? In sports? In your first job? In anything?

Nobody starts at the top in politics either.

You can skip the rungs that are too simplistic for your experience; jump on the ladder at as high a rung as you can handle.

A first rung for beginners is to *become an active on-location government spectator.* Get up to city council meetings. Watch. Learn. You'll be amazed at how few others are watching over your most precious asset, your freedom.

A good second rung is to *start a watch committee* with a handful of neighbors to go with you so the council becomes aware that there is always a delegation from your neighborhood—watching. That alone improves council performance.

Meanwhile, your neighbors learn. It always amazes them. Most never know, for example, what constitutes so-called "emergency legislation." They quickly learn that classifying a bill as "emergency" allows the council to bypass a lot of good procedure and outflank the public.

These are only two samples of several dozen ploys to learn en route to professional citizenship. Educated spectators worry council into better action.

. . . . and it is so far true. . . that the same tyranny which drove the first emigrants from home pursues their descendants still.
—Common Sense

A logical third rung—*broaden the surveillance to other local government meetings:* the planning commission, zoning board, board of appeals, charter commission, utility commission, water board, sewer committee, and all the boards in town. If you are running out of people, get each club or lodge in town to assign specific monitoring committees. Mere citizen presence corrects many deficiencies, such as the presence of builders on the zoning boards, pipe contractors on the sewer committee, cement salesmen on the roads committee.

Note whether committee action seems cut and dried, as if predecided in a previous private meeting. This is illegal but common, a technique of ball control by the pros. Raise hell about it.

Men who look upon themselves born to reign and others to obey soon grow insolent. Selected from the rest of mankind, their minds are early poisoned by importance.

—Common Sense

A well-informed group in the audience commands attention. The key is well-informed. Your government recognizes knowledgeability. That's a worry.

A fourth rung—*get on one of these boards or committees.* No pay, but it's the route to the inside of your government. You build clout. There is a government web at all levels. Get in it.

That doesn't appeal to you? Don't do it. There is a fifth rung that is not quite governmental but still provides a strong foothold on your local government. Join a favorite local quasi-official body—your school board advisory committee, friends of the library, the hospital board. These put you into liaison with government. So do the town chamber of commerce and various service and philanthropical organizations. You earn credits around town; you are not just a voter. The local government must deal with you. You are becoming a force.

A sixth rung—*join a local political club:* Young Democrats, Young Republicans, League of Women Voters, or others. Get on the inside.

A seventh rung—*make a run for council yourself.* Win or lose, you are developing muscle with local government figures.

An eighth rung—*move on up.* The steps just described for town and city also apply to county and state.

A good opening move at the state level is to organize a watch committee to travel to the state capital to observe your representative and state senator in action. (Yes, it costs money. Freedom was never free.) You may find that your representative is not attending sessions, is not on any committees, and is altogether out of it. That means you are not really represented.

At the state level, educate yourself on a whole new group of ploys. For example, learn the budgetary dangers of lame duck legislative sessions. There is a whole playbook to be learned en route to becoming a professional citizen. Get started, and at a level that enlists your enthusiasm and ability.

After you have learned some ropes, you will find government starts paying attention. You are now someone they must consider.

Ash-haired George W. Salay, in his seventies, helps his wife, Virginia, get the supper dishes done a little early Monday night, then drives up to council meeting in Garfield Heights, Ohio (population 34,500). Some snowy nights it is not so easy. But he has done this every alternate Monday for more than a dozen years.

The councilmen look up and nod when Salay walks in. They are not all that glad to see him, but they know he will be informed on everything they will discuss tonight.

Some townsmen say Salay is a nuisance; others say he is the stabilizer of the community's politics. The politicians know he can quickly alert and mobilize a large cadre of citizens on any issue. "And he *will*," explained one councilman. "That's where his strength lies. We *know* he will *act*."

That says it all. *They know he will act.*

Can you imagine our strength if in every small city there were even one hundred George Salays?—one hundred people about whom it is known *they will act?*

Yes, it costs, either in effort or money. Freedom is not free.

Master the Techniques of the Pros

As the citizen grows in professional savvy, he becomes effective. Here are some of the kinds of things he learns.

He learns to beware of *co-optation*, a device of governments to disarm probable opponents. They take the opposition into the fold, making an opponent part of the operation, "the citizen adviser" or some such. Thus, if influential Ms. Ego is likely to object to locating the new fire station in the middle of Arboretum Park, she's invited onto the citizen advisory board. There she can be flattered, handled, or out-voted...and thus destroyed.

Join those boards, but be alert.

The professional citizen learns the power of demonstration.

In Bryan, Ohio, the State of Ohio was already rolling in big earthmoving equipment to widen quiet, lovely Main Street, where the trees meet over the street. The contractors were going to make it part of a state route. The town government and the State of Ohio wanted it, and they had the necessary enabling papers signed.

The townspeople did not want the street widened. It meant cutting down a grand concourse of beautiful trees. The citizen group opposed to this destruction campaigned earnestly but naively for a year. . . and they lost. The dozers rolled in.

Men who look upon themselves born to reign and others to obey soon grow insolent. . .poisoned by importance.

—Common Sense

And then a politically aware high school science teacher set his class to work nights researching the dollar value of the different types of trees on Main Street for both landscaping and lumber. On a Sunday, as people came downtown to church, they saw the trees astride Main Street each wearing a large weatherproof value sign, ranging from $750 to $3,080.

People drove slowly, adding up the signs, amazed at the dollar value, realizing that value was about to be subtracted from the community's assets. Leaving aside the merits or demerits of the highway, the point is that the demonstration worked. The citizens besieged the statehouse. The bulldozers were called off.

The professional citizen also employs ridicule shrewdly.

Don Pierce, seventeen, Canby, Oregon, received notification from the IRS that an investigator would come to his parents' house to audit his income tax return. Don's father, Mike Pierce, protested the "tremendous waste of taxpayer money" to audit the teenager's papers—two W-2 forms attached to the standard short form. Don had earned $1,772.26 and was due a refund.

The IRS insisted on the audit. Mike Pierce advised the media and sent the resulting news clips to Washington. On Monday, November 17, 1980, an ABC-TV network film crew sat in Don Pierce's house ready to film this big audit. District IRS director, Ralph Short, phoned Pierce. His Washington office had wired orders suspending all audits of this nature.

Bureaucracy worries about egg on its face.

While the average humble phone call or letter to legislators is dismissed as "not worth a damn," the professional citizen learns to make it work. How?

There is a wealth of printed material on this subject, but for example, if you get a brush-off reply from an official, publish it in letters to the editor. If the brush-off is egregious, send a photocopy to several letters-to-editor columns.

The high-level politician subscribes to clipping services. His name printed in your letter to the editor does get his attention. Sooner or later someone on his staff says, "Hey, Senator, we'd better see what this character is all about." Also, his party leaders decide they had better look.

An eleven-year-old girl wrote to Cuyahoga County Engineer Albert S. Porter begging for the repair of a long-closed Berea, Ohio, bridge that daily detoured the citizens at great cost. For twenty years, this powerful politician had run an arrogant administration, staying in office with the help of a famous employee-supported Flower Fund. Repeated newspaper investigations failed to dislodge him.

Porter wrote the girl a scolding, insulting, and haughty reply.

The young lady broke into tears. Then, with guidance, she made a simple move with profound result—she mailed Porter's reply to the newspaper for publication just before the election. Porter's twenty-year career crumbled.

The same technique also brings results when, in your opinion, a politician is doing something well. Send letters of approval to the press and to his party leadership.

Take individual action, but also join with like-minded others. Build your mob. Your influence is proportional to the numbers you represent. Use your clubs and organizations. Rally the membership around your cause to muster numbers power. Politicians are in the numbers games.

You may need to build a mob from several towns. Barbara Surwilo of Rocky Hill, Connecticut, needed some help. Back in 1973, federal highway planners announced that an interstate would soon shoot high-speed traffic straight through her neighborhood.

Barbara disagreed. But instead of fighting it just with a local anesthetic, she organized ad hoc committees in other communities on the interstate's announced route. It took six years. . . and nine thousand hours of Barbara's time. But she won.

Individuals can operate the system rapidly when they employ knowledgeable professionalism.

Two young Cities Service Company employees, Ken Thomas and Bill Wright, discovered an error in the 1976 Oklahoma tax law, which omitted child-care expenses as a deductible credit, significantly raising taxes for some people. They set out to correct this, not with amateur rhetoric and flailing around. They mobilized young people's clubs, TV public opinion shows, and letter campaigns to all key legislators. It took only one month and one day to get a corrective emergency bill passed.

Form a citizen action bloc. It can be powerful. Donald K. Ross's book, *A Public Citizen's Action Manual*, blueprints how to do this.

Enlist newspapers. Our public officials and bureaus operate behind a screen of public ignorance.

Persuade local newspapers to run prominent and regular features on the voting records of city, state, and federal lawmakers. The effect is not so much on the public as on the legislators.

These big ones are at the top of the list of citizen techniques.

Use popular initiative and referendum. But they require real professionalism, and citizens need more practice with them.

When representative government fails to represent, the two formal procedures of initiative and referendum are often available to us. Making them work is a massive job, but it can be done. They would work better if they were worked more often. Californians, who brought off Proposition 13 to reduce property taxes 57 percent, successfully used the techniques of initiative and referendum.

Michael Nelson, in "Power to the People," *Saturday Review*, November 1979, revealed that in the '70s some 175 initiatives were successfully brought to vote at state level, almost twice as many as in the '60s, when the direct-action politics of mass demonstrations and marches was in vogue.

It can be made to work if we work at it.

The Most Important
Freedom Action Front
in the World

Your children are it. To correct the mistakes of the generations who gave up citizen control of government, bring up your children differently.

Youth is the seedtime of good habits, as well in nations as in individuals.
                                                    —Common Sense

"Too slow," you say. No. An eleven-year-old boy and girl become man and woman in one fleeting decade.

If you ever doubt a parent can affect the course of history, consider Rose Kennedy. The Kennedy boys did not just wake up one morning and decide to go into government. That idea was planted by their parents before the boys outgrew their training wheels. Mealtime for the kids meant contributing to the conversation about current affairs.

Revive in your children the forgotten concept that they are the government. Take them regularly to city and county and state legislatures, so they feel like owners of their government, not guests.

Especially instill an awesome respect for the vote.

Let them see you laboring to select your candidates.

Too many voters grab the newspaper the day of the election and try to study the issues and candidates in twenty minutes. Entering the voting booth with encyclopedic ignorance, they turn to outrageous criteria—"Sounds like a good Irish name."

Urging a big vote turnout by an uninformed electorate—is that a good thing? Maybe yes. Maybe no. It is arguable.

But you will have children and friends who doubt a single vote really matters, even if informed. Does one vote have any clout?

Your vote counts. It is a very worn cliche, but important: In 1928, Franklin Delano Roosevelt was elected governor of New York by a margin of about two votes per precinct. That changed the course of history. Lyndon Baines Johnson won a run-off election in Texas for a U.S. Senate seat by only 87 votes—a margin of .0145 of a vote per precinct. In 1948, if only one Truman voter in each precinct in Ohio and California had stayed away from the polls, Dewey would have captured fifty more electoral votes. Truman would have lost fifty, and the election would have gone into the House of Representatives. In 1960, John F. Kennedy's national plurality was equal to about one-half of one vote per precinct.

Yet voter turnout continues to diminish as a percentage of those eligible. In 1976, only 38 percent of those under twenty voted, half the ratio of those over thirty-five. In the 1978 election, an estimated two-thirds of all eligible voters left their destiny in the hands of the other third of the voters. A *New York Times* story published the day after the 1980 election confirmed that one major group of nonvoters continues to be the young.

But, by abdicating our right to govern, we leave a vacuum in which government grows and spends, secretly using our money, taking on illegal authority, and reducing individual freedom.

Ye that oppose independence now, ye know not what ye do; ye are opening a door to eternal tyranny. . . .

—Common Sense

Inflation can be rather quickly stopped. The dollar can gradually again be a full-value sound dollar. The politician can be made honest—he needs your vote or he is out of a job.

Big government must have our big money and our big vote to exist.

Never abdicate.

O ye that love mankind! Ye that dare oppose not only the tyranny but the tyrant, stand forth! Every spot of the Old World is overrun with oppression. Freedom has been hunted round the globe. Asia and Africa have long expelled her. Europe regards her like a stranger, and England has given her warning to depart. O! receive the fugitive, and prepare in time an asylum for mankind.

—Common Sense

9

More!

*A Walk in the Woods of Democracy
with Mr. Lincoln*

The trouble with liberty is that it's temporary.

The trouble with government is that it's permanent.

They are natural enemies. One is always trying to destroy the other. If government wins, it's tyranny. If liberty wins, it's chaos.

We need a balanced stand-off. Do the preceding chapters show a common sense way to achieve that? Let us bring in an outside expert to review.

Who?

Although Thomas Paine first made famous the phase *common sense,* can you think of anyone whose leadership it better describes than Abraham Lincoln's?

While Paine was the master of the logic of *obtaining* freedom, Abraham Lincoln, in America's second make-or-break crisis nine decades later, became the common sense master of *sustaining* freedom.

Both Paine and the Great Emancipator fed the freedom-starved parts of the world a nourishing diet of ideas on liberty so that they became the two most hungrily read political Americans around the globe. Their words are still the world textbook for freedom, enduring to this day in the political action literature of all continents.

In today's third internal great crisis of freedom, Lincoln's logic proves timeless, beginning with his message to Congress on July 4, 1861: "Surely each man has as strong a motive now to preserve our liberties as each had then [in the Revolution]to establish them."[1] He knew then the great hazard which we ignore: "It has long been a grave question whether any government, not too strong for the liberties of its people, can be strong enough to maintain its existence in great emergencies."[2]

We need to approach the problem as scared as Lincoln was. We saw in Chapter 1 that what big government strives to help, it hurts. What it tries to save, it kills. Power derived from the people raises itself above the people. Lincoln worried about that, too, as he worked to balance freedom and sovereignty:

This issue [the Civil War] embraces more than the fate of these United States. . . . It forces us to ask, is there in all republics this inherent and fatal weakness? Must a government of necessity be too strong for the liberties of its own people or too weak to maintain its own existence?[3]

In Chapter 1 we saw excessive, coercive, and contradictory regulatory policy today becoming the single greatest brake on American innovation. General freedom begins dissolving with the first dilution of personal economic independence. The once sound American dollar has been diluted in value since 1934 to where it now buys only a dime's worth. We are being robbed of the liberty to plan our individual lives.

To avoid national disaster, this erosion of value must be stopped, then gradually reversed. With high productivity, the soundness of the dollar can gradually be restored, along with our freedom. Strong incentive for both individual initiative and private concern for the well-being of others can accomplish this if we reduce the load of big government to a bare minimum. As Lincoln observed, "If our American Society and the United States government are demoralized and overthrown, it will come from the voracious desire for office, this wriggle to live without toil, work and labor. . .from which I am not free myself."[4]

We do have the tools—first of all, the vote. Big government needs both big votes and big money to survive. Lincoln knew that: "It is not the qualified voters, but the qualified voters *who choose to vote,* that constitute the political power of the state."[5]

A second powerful tool we need to support is the sunset law, including limits to judicial tenure. Lincoln anticipated that, too: "Nothing should ever be implied by law which leads to unjust or absurd consequences."[6]

In these pages, we have seen the common-sense facts of life about wage raises, namely that viable raises can come from only one source, increased productivity. Lincoln understood this even as a young politician as early as 1847.

> . . . *the habits of our whole species fall into three great classes—useful labor, useless labor, and idleness. Of these the first only is meritorious, and to it all the products of labor rightfully belong; but the two latter, while they exist, are heavy pensioners upon the first, robbing it of a large portion of its rights. The only remedy for this is to, as far as possible, drive useless labor and idleness out.*[7]

The practical route to higher pay is working smarter and innovating. Lincoln was so sure of this that in a debate in Galesburg in 1858 he risked telling possibly the most revolting story in all political folklore. It makes a graphic point.

> *The fisherman's wife whose drowned husband was brought home with his body full of eels, said when she was asked what was to be done with him, "Take out the eels and set him again."*[8]

Productivity works positively on both inflation and recession, increasing real wages. What free men need is not more inflated paper dollars, but more buying power.

One step to that is a more productive use of resources now allocated to government. As we've observed, monopolies are difficult to make productive. Government is a monopoly. To increase productivity, we should remove from government those services that could be handled by private contractors. Twenty years ago the U.S. Post Office handled about 800 million packages, while United Parcel Service delivered 100 million. Today the Postal Service delivers 200 million annually while UPS delivers over a billion.

Worse, however, big government habitually makes regulations that destroy the productivity of others. Lincoln had something to say about that, too: "As labor is the common burden of our race, so the effort of some to shift their share of the burden onto the shoulders of others is a great durable curse of the race."[9] And today that effort is largely governmental in nature.

High productivity lowers costs, increases sales, making high employment. High labor costs prevent competing in world markets, leading to unemployment. That is dangerous. Lincoln saw that already in the middle of that last century. "No country can sustain in idleness more than a small percentage of its numbers. The great majority must labor at something productive."[10]

Lincoln was not against the right to strike. He recognized the value of a free market in labor: "I am glad to see that a system of labor prevails in New England under which laborers can strike when they want to...I like the system which lets a man quit when he wants to and wish it might prevail everywhere."[11]

But a free market in labor provides no right to prevent others from doing the work. To quote Lincoln again, "I believe each individual is naturally entitled to do as he pleases with himself and the fruit of his labor, so far as it no wise interferes with any other men's rights."[12] By extension, the government employee charged with our security should no more have the right to strike than a uniformed infantryman. That kind of strike interferes with the public's rights.

We have seen how minimum wage laws discriminate against low-skill people, barring them from the first rung of the career ladder. Child labor laws first protected children from working in cold dangerous mines. Today, these expanded laws "protect" young people from working in air-conditioned offices.

Minorities do not need special programs. They do need to have big government stop blocking their opportunities. As Lincoln observed, "There is no permanent class of hired laborers amongst us. Twenty-five years ago I was a hired laborer. The hired laborer of yesterday labors on his own account today, and will hire others to labor for him tomorrow."[13]

In Chapters 2 and 3, we saw workingmen often knowing more about running a business than the restrictive relationship with management now allows them to contribute. Workingmen have not yet much considered the fact that they own voting control of many corporations via their pension funds. With that, plus profit sharing, both management and labor have reason to pull in the same direction, creating *real* raises via raising the buying power of the dollar. "No men living are more worthy to be trusted than those who toil up from poverty," Lincoln observed common-sensically.[14]

Two good ways to measure progress in getting more buying power in our pay (reducing inflation) are to monitor the cost of the market basket and the dollars needed to buy gold coins.

In Chapter 3 we also saw the cruelty of welfare. Begun out of kindness, it now cruelly locks people into the feudalistic kind of dependence and poverty that men fought a thousand years to escape. The United States, erstwhile bastion of self-reliance and independence, has converted itself eagerly with the help of vote-hungry leaders into the world's largest welfare state.

Devastating as the dollar cost may be, a greater cost is to national character. The resultant massive erosion of freedom, human dignity, self-reliance, self-respect, personal pride, and honor undercuts our foundations. It is a bobsled run straight into bondage. The continuing transfer of income from producers to nonproducers destroys the work incentive of both and creates mutual disrespect. We should heed the wisdom of Lincoln: "Let us at all times remember that all American citizens are brothers of a common country, and should dwell together in the bonds of fraternal feeling."[15]

A negative income tax would better help the people and in the most useful form—cash—halting the erosion of individual freedom. It should be as automatic as the present income tax, replacing the existing welfare system with its expensive paperwork industry and nonproductive army of bureaucrats.

It would not be fair for those receiving negative income tax funds to vote during that time, but the franchise would reactivate immediately when the citizen became a taxpayer. We agree with Lincoln:

I go for all *sharing the privileges of the government who assist in bearing its burdens. Consequently, I go for admitting all. . . to the right of suffrage who pay taxes or bear arms—by no means excluding females.*[16]

In Chapter 1 we saw the Frenchman Alexis de Tocqueville warn, "This young republic will probably endure until its politicians learn that its people can be bribed with their own money." Lincoln warned us of that as well. "In my opinion, there is not a more foolish or demoralizing way of conducting political rivalry than these fierce and bitter struggles for patronage."[17]

And that brings us to the Social Security boondoggle, where everyone is promised more cake than we have available to eat. It is common sense that a viable system must replace Social Security before it destroys itself and us.

Social Security, sold to the people and the Congress as a minimum safety net, has grown into a whole way of life, an effort to patronize everybody. The entire federal Social Security system, including medical and unemployment benefit programs, could and should be phased out and replaced by the simple negative income tax, including powerful, substantial tax deduction incentives for saving. As Lincoln urged the Committee of Workingmen's Association of New York on March 21, 1864, "Let not him who is houseless pull down the houses of another, but let him work diligently and build one for himself, thus by example assuring that his own shall be safe from violence when built."[18]

Allowable income tax deductions for individual retirement and emergencies should be expanded into powerful rewards for saving. Deducting from taxable income the full amount saved up to twenty percent of income, *plus an additional* twenty percent of the saving, would make a very strong incentive for individual saving for future security. Savings in government administration costs should far exceed the revenue lost by the twenty percent deductible incentive.

However, any money saved by the citizen is false security unless the melting of its dollar value is halted and gradually reversed.

Of course, even with this reformed system in place, certainly there would still be human emergencies to be handled. But we've seen that compassionate volunteerism can come up with the troops to do the job. We simply need to build in the incentive. We can install a powerful reward for charitably solving extreme hardship through citizen action, stimulating concern for others. Allow income tax deduction of the full amount of charitable gifts up to twenty percent of income, *plus* another twenty percent of the gift itself. The twin 20/20 plans for individual saving and for charitable giving will create strong, thrifty, compassionate citizenship. It's not only a means of meeting essential hardship needs. It stimulates and nourishes individual independence. Lincoln said, "Destroy this spirit of liberty and you have planted the seeds of despotism at your doors. . . . you have lost the genius of your own independence and become fit subjects of the first cunning tyrant who rises among you."[19]

But notice another huge advantage. The citizens' entire income affairs are thus handled by a single device, the simplified income tax administered by a single staff, instead of being handled by a multiplicity of huge complex systems and bureaus.

In Chapter 4 we saw excessive governmental regulation loading ever heavier costs onto the taxpayer's back, leading to the destruction of United States as a democracy. The citizen has become the servant of government rather than the reverse. But Lincoln reminds us, "The people of these United States are the rightful masters of both congresses and courts, not to overthrow the Constitution, but to overthrow the men who pervert the Constitution."[20]

Recognizing this, we proposed two actions regarding any regulatory agencies needed.

First, whenever feasible, they should be taken over from the government and administered and financed by those who create the need for them or benefit from them. Lincoln understood that these bureaus grow like pigweed in a wet summer. He warned one officeholder, "I understand a bill is before congress, by your instigation, for taking your office from control of the department of the Interior, and considerably enlarging the powers and patronage of your office.... If the change is made, I do not think I can allow you to retain the office, because that would be encouraging officers to be constantly intriguing, to the detriment of the public interest, in order to profit themselves."[21]

Years earlier, in a speech in Congress given June 30, 1848, he warned, "The tendency to undue expansion is unquestionably the chief difficulty. How to do something, and still not too much, is the desideratum."[22]

Our second conclusion is that, if found necessary and unavoidable, the regulatory agency should be administered by a governmental agency—*but paid for* by the recipients of the service. As Lincoln stated in a speech in the Illinois Legislature on January 11, 1837, "It is an old maxim and a very sound one that he that dances should always pay the fiddler. Now, sir, if any gentlemen, whose money is a burden to them, choose to lead off a dance, I am decidedly opposed to the peoples' money being used to pay the fiddler."[23] And so are we. And so, we suspect, are you.

If neither the first nor second solution occurs, then the agency should be phased out completely in three years.

Nearly every government service worth keeping can be self-financing. But a first principle to follow is, "In all that the people can individually do as well for themselves, government ought not to interfere."[24]

In Chapter 5 we noted the government's attack on the people by not maintaining an honest dollar.

We believe with Lincoln that "No duty is more imperative on... government than the duty it owes the people of furnishing them a sound and uniform currency."[25]

We did not stay on guard nor understand the consequences of 1934. That year the government banged the gold door shut to Americans. That in turn opened the door to inflation and loss of liberty.

Inflation is hidden taxation without representation.

There are two kinds of money, Type I and Type C. Both are important, but they are opposites. *Invested* money increases productivity and cuts inflation. *Consumed* money—that is, money that is eaten, worn, drunk, or wasted—inflates prices.

When savings are high (Type I), interest rates quickly drop to the true rate (2 percent to 3 percent), plus a factor for any uncertainty in the future of the economy and a factor for risks that apply to a specific borrower. . . . plus the rate of inflation. With an inflationary economy, the usually dependable bond market (where people save for retirement) becomes a gambling casino.

To return to the true interest rate (2 percent to 3 percent), reduce spendthrift big government to a bare minimum. Then the government itself will once again be able to borrow at "the true rate of interest." The bond market will regain its former high-grade quality. The dollar will become a consistently strong currency.

Creating additional money because big government spends more than it receives is a tremendous hidden tax on citizens, imposed without their instruction or knowledge—a giant unseen step to tyranny.

Inflation turns a nation around philosophically: from savers to spenders; from producers to consumers; ultimately from free men to welcomers of absolute government control.

Lenders to government who received government's high interest this year will be paid back later in money with still less buying power. Nobody will win but big government. It is an old saying but true—spending our way out of inflation is like trying to drink ourselves sober.

For several years past the revenues of the government have been unequal to its expenditures, and consequently loan after loan. . . . has been resorted to. By this means a new national debt has been created, and is still growing on us with a rapidity fearful to contemplate. . . . . The present debt must be paid. . . . The system of loans. . . must soon explode. . . . As an individual who undertakes to live by borrowing soon finds his original means devoured by interest, and next, no one left to borrow from, so it must be with a government. "[26]

Lincoln said that in a Whig circular already on March 4, 1843.

The best-kept secret about debt is apparently so technically complex that sophisticated MBAs cannot quite grasp it. Yet we've found that the common citizen understands the basic axiom just fine. Mrs. McGuire explains it: "The whole thing about debt is. . .sooner or later somebody's got to pay." Only big government could be so oblivious to the obvious. Balancing the budget is basic to solving the nation's monetary (high interest) problem.

In Chapter 5 we showed the steps by which inflation, price controls, and high taxes drive trade underground.

Big government's big sneak inflation tax begets big sneak tax evasion. A huge market develops in untraceable, untaxable cash exchange and barter, now estimated at between $200 and $300 billion a year.

The compounding inflation rate has been approaching a flash point. Unless we set affairs to right soon, big government must take over totally to allocate diminishing resources. To do this, big government will need force. That is the end of democracy.

The voter must charge his elected deputies to win back the sound U.S. dollar—furnish tax incentives to save; encourage citizens to implement their concern for the well-being of others by tax incentives for their charitable giving, thereby lowering the government's welfare cost; and reduce government to a bare minimum.

We can make another move with tremendous potential. National productivity would explode if we eliminated big government's tax incentive for corporate waste by killing the triple-dip corporation income tax. Corporations do not really pay the tax; they only pass it on. In the first dip, stockholders pay corporation income taxes as owners of the business. On the second dip, stockholders next pay personal income taxes on the corporation dividends they receive. On the third dip, stockholders and everyone else pay the higher prices of more inflation.

We must further recognize that efficient corporate management is stimulated by competition and free trade. Both are very effective price controls and the only ones needed. Government price and production control must be discouraged. Big government's price controls actually raise prices by slowing competitive developments.

Abolishing the corporation income tax will turn a stream of seed money into industry, creating more productivity, more employment, more value in the dollar.

Income taxes must be paid directly, obviously, and honestly by taxpaying citizens. They should not be hidden by taxing a piece of paper called a corporation which only passes on the tax to consumers. Financial author Gary Allen once counted 152 taxes in a loaf of bread. That's about 10 per slice. When citizens tolerate hidden taxes, they have lost control of their government.

How can we see if we are making progress in raising the real value of the dollar? The same way we see inflation—by monitoring the monthly cost of the market basket and the quoted dollar price of U.S. minted gold medallions. For the latter, phone the post office. Simple.

From 1930 to 1981, the price of $5.00 worth of necessities inflated to approximately $50.00, giving us a 10-cent dollar.

Self-reliance, creative effort, and working smartly to achieve increased productivity of goods and services, *plus* close monitoring of big government's expenditures, can accomplish the basic long-range (sixty-year) objective—raising the present 10-cent dollar to its former 100-cent value. At that time the gold standard should be adopted to assure future sound currency.

Shays' armed rebellion, responding to an arrogant government then run by judges who were destroying the currency, came very close to destroying our new democracy. But you cannot force a free people to accept phony money. As Lincoln wrote to John J. Crittenden (December 22, 1859), "No law is stronger than is the public sentiment where it is to be enforced."[27] He also observed in a debate on October 7, 1858, "Jefferson said that judges are as honest as other men and not more so. And he said, substantially, that whenever a free people should give up in absolute submission to any department of government, retaining for themselves no appeal from it, their liberties were gone."[28]

Where is our appeal against the tyrannous tax of government-induced inflation? Taxes are necessary. But one thing people must enforce: Taxes must be *visible*—never hidden pickpocket taxation. Why should citizens be honest when their government is dishonest?

Visible federal consumption taxes (except on necessity goods) may be needed in addition to federal taxes on personal income. "It is fair that each man shall pay taxes in exact proportion to the value of his property...."[29] Taxes on incomes, however, should probably be limited to 30 percent to preserve individual initiative and avoid encouraging the underground economy.

In Chapter 6 we noted that there is presently an untapped source of potentially increased productivity. Government, owner of nearly a fourth of the U.S. land mass, could sell or lease appropriate lands so that natural resources become available. This should include the requirements that these lands be returned to the equivalent condition, or better, after use.

The immense mineral resources of some of these [American] territories ought to be developed as rapidly as possible. Every step in that direction would have a tendency to improve the revenues of the government, and diminish the burdens of the people. It is worthy of your serious consideration whether some extraordinary measures to promote that end cannot be adopted.[30]

And for more fiscal productivity on the part of government services now rendered free should be paid directly by those users. "Particularity—expending the money of the whole people for an object which will benefit only a portion of them—is the greatest objection to [internal] improvements."[31]

Chapter 7 claimed a fourth basic necessity of life—education. If we are to retain freedom in a complex world, education is now a necessity.

We are proposing solo learning. Teach all our children to teach themselves in school as our graduate students do, with top rate guidance and innovative, interesting, stimulating educational equipment. Moving the solo learning concept to elementary and high school grades could create a nation of powerful, effective citizens who possess the key to whatever they want to do in life—the ability to teach themselves, the ability to adapt to change. What Lincoln said remains true: "In a word, free labor insists on universal education."[32] "...in this country one can scarcely be so poor but that, if he will, he can acquire sufficient education...."[33]

Solo learning can be a breakthrough to extra-quality mass education. The best education budgets today can usually only furnish one teacher for twenty students. What a release from this restrictive ratio to suddenly have twenty self-teachers in a class, guided by one professional teacher!

Foreign relations are similar to personal relations.

Put a good man on a dole with gifts that make him dependent

and indebted, you diminish his self-respect, competence, and independence. . .and he resents you.

The solutions to the problems of emerging nations will best come from within these countries, assisted by us with trade and friendly know-how, not cash.

America's most effective method of spreading human rights around the world is to sustain the world's best example here. Individual freedom and prosperity are related. That is democratic strength. President Carter put it powerfully—"The great democracies are not free because they are rich. They are rich because they are free."

We best serve the world by perfecting the democratic model in our own house. Successful intervention in the internal affairs of foreign nations is probably beyond the skills of even the best state department in the world over the long term.

Having said that, nevertheless, given the nuclear threat overhead, it is common sense that the United States now needs to become the most proficient international negotiator in history, firm but benevolent.

Many feel that our best posture in doing that is maintaining even-handed respect for all nations, avoiding commercial partiality, letting free competition operate, using tariff duties only as necessary to escape catastrophic trade imbalances. In the long term, free international trade competition creates the best economics and the best diplomacy.

We want to see today's government honor the promise Lincoln made in his inaugural speech on March 4, 1861: "The power confided in me will be used to hold, occupy, and possess the property and places belonging to the government, and to collect the duties and imposts; but beyond what may be necessary for these objects, there will be no invasion, no using of force against or among the people anywhere."[34]

We do have big enemies: hostile nations and internal organized crime.

Defense *is* the correct role of government.

Put solid force on display; you seldom have to use it.

The ideal U.S. national defense policy is probably a strong military force backed by a strong economy backed by a strong citizenry.

Democratic strength, with its release of the creative initiative of millions of people, is the best foundation for military strength. "The people when they rise in mass in behalf of the Union and the liberties of their country, truly may it be said, 'the gates of hell cannot prevail against them.' "[35]

Will the strengthening of our military be at the expense of social programs? Is it common sense to believe that U.S. social programs can survive if the United States does not?

Our nation's strength and policy must be clear to our friends and to our opponents, including internal enemies. And our defense must include a defense of principles.

"Reason—cold, calculating, unimpassioned reason—must furnish all the materials for our future support and defense. Let those materials be molded into general intelligence, sound morality, and in particular a reverence for the Constitution and laws."[36]

Beyond that, how we treat the other guy is crucial. A strong tax-saving incentive creating compassionate citizenship is the correct reply to the Hobbesian theory of mankind's natural selfishness. The better we treat each other, the less government we need, the less taxes, the less inflation, the more freedom. We echo the words of the Great Emancipator: "I hold that while man exists it is his duty to improve not only his own condition, but to assist in ameliorating mankind. I am for those means which will give the greatest good to the greatest number."[37]

Where Have We Been?

The three of us—you and Ray Armington and Bill Ellis—have had the presumption to take this walk through the woods of democracy and discuss some profound subjects. But free citizens *must* have that presumption in order to do the job as outlined in Chapter 8. By constitutional authority, we are supposed to be the boss. We cannot wholly delegate the consideration of principle to the government people on our payroll or we're dead.

We must rouse ourselves. The *only* way we will win back freedom and a sound dollar from big government will be by huge numbers of us shedding our dangerous indifference to apply intensive, clamorous, insistent citizen pressure on those who presume to be speaking for us when they tell us what to do.

The solutions the three of us have been exploring, devising a road map back to freedom, have not just been the thoughts of alarmed amateurs. They reflect the convictions of a corps of distinguished political scientists and economists. See the suggested reading list in the appendix.

Then why add *this* book? Because these experts generally have not been addressing the public-at-large so much as other professionals. But it is we the public who must finally drive the action. That's why we the authors asked you to join us for a walk through that forest of opinion, to lay out a trail for the trip back to freedom.

Thanks for coming.

The trip back has already begun, but to reach the goal requires a very clear road map and a large insistent crowd who knows the route.

Build that crowd.

You will encounter indifference and resistance. You will encounter heated, wordy agreement cooled by immediate inaction.

Fall back on the common sense of it: The better we treat the other guy, the better off we are, the less government we need, the less taxes we pay, the less inflation we spawn, the more freedom we earn.

All-out grass roots action will move us along the route to get and keep *more*, will lead us to the heritage we came too close to losing—freedom.

NOTES

The Lincoln quotations are taken from *The Lincoln Encyclopedia* by Archer H. Shaw, published by The Macmillan Company, New York, 1950. They can also be found in the volumes published by Francis D. Tandy Company, New York, 1905. We've provided page references to both for reader convenience.

1. From Lincoln's message to Congress, July 4, 1861: Archer H. Shaw, *The Lincoln Encyclopedia*, Macmillan, New York, 1950, p. 188. Francis D. Tandy Company, New York, 1905, Vol. VI, p. 312.

2. Shaw, p. 293; Tandy, Vol. X, p. 264.

3. Shaw, p. 292; Tandy, Vol. VI, p. 304.

4. Lincoln to W. H. Herndon: Shaw, p. 233 (Robert Todd Lincoln papers).

5. Lincoln's opinion on admission of West Virginia to the Union, Dec. 31, 1862: Shaw, p. 234; Tandy, Vol. VIII, p. 157.

6. Lincoln to Congress, July 4, 1861: Shaw, p. 183; Tandy, Vol. VI, p. 317.

7. Lincoln's Tariff Memorandum, Dec. 1, 1847: Shaw, p. 181; Tandy, Vol. I, p. 307.

8. Lincoln's debate at Galesburg, Oct. 7, 1858: Shaw, p. 152; Tandy, Vol. IV, p. 279.

9. Shaw, p. 152; Tandy, Vol. II, p. 185.

10. Shaw, p. 156; Tandy, Vol. V, p. 251.

11. Shaw, p. 179; Tandy, Vol. V, p. 360.

12. Shaw, p. 160; Tandy, Vol. III, p. 35.

13. Lincoln fragment, July 1, 1854: Shaw, p. 179; Tandy, Vol. II, p. 184.

14. Shaw, p. 255.

15. Shaw, p. 10; Tandy, Vol. VI, p. 72.

16. Shaw, p. 389; Tandy, Vol. I, p. 14.

17. Shaw, p. 236; Tandy, Vol. X, p. 101.

18. Shaw, p. 152; Tandy, Vol. X, p. 54.

19. Shaw, p. 78; Tandy, Vol. XI, p. 110.

20. Shaw, p. 242; Tandy, Vol. V, p. 232.

21. Shaw, p. 163; Tandy, Vol. X, p. 56.

22. Shaw, p. 163; Tandy, Vol. V, p. 46.

23. Shaw, p. 118.

24. Shaw, p. 136; Tandy, Vol. II, p. 87.

25. Shaw, p. 20; Tandy, Vol. I, p. 110.

26. Shaw, p. 221; Tandy, Vol. I, p. 245.

27. Shaw, p. 183.

28. Shaw, p. 169; Tandy, Vol. V, p. 286.

29. Shaw, p. 351; Tandy, Vol. X, p. 200.

30. Shaw, p. 210; Tandy, Vol. VIII, p. 100.

31. Shaw, p. 162; Tandy, Vol. II, p. 44.

32. Shaw, p. 178; Tandy, Vol. V, p. 252.

33. Shaw, p. 94; Tandy, Vol. II, p. 160.

34. Shaw, p. 163; Tandy, Vol. VI, p. 175.

35. Shaw, p. 132; Tandy, Vol. II, p. 111.

36. Shaw, p. 266; Tandy, Vol. I, p. 50.

37. Shaw, p. 136; Tandy, Vol. VI, p. 120.

Appendix

Where to Write for Help
in Becoming a Professional Citizen

- For analyses of Congessional voting records, write:

    The Americans for Constitutional Action
    995 L'Enfant Plaza North, S.W., Suite 1000
    Washington, D.C.   20024

- To subscribe to *The Congressional Record,* write:

    Government Printing Office
    North Capitol Street
    Washington, D.C.   20402
    (Cost $45/year)

- For advice and legal assistance in getting information from
  the government, write:

    Freedom of Information Clearinghouse
    P.O. Box 19367
    Washington, D.C.   20036

- For information on education reform, write:

    Council for Basic Education
    725 15th Street, N.W.
    Washington, D.C.   20005

- For voting/attendance records of local, county, or state legislators, contact your local, county, or state agency, body,
  house, whatever. They do not print records, but can supply
  the information.

- For instructions on organizing a state lobby, write:

  The Citizen Action Group
  2000 P Street, N.W.
  Washington, D.C.   20036

- For information on laws governing an initiative action in your state, contact the Secretary of State in your capital city.

- To determine which agency in Washington is the one to seek help or advice for your business or interest, contact:

  The Office of Business Liaison, Room 1510
  Commerce Department
  Washington, D.C.   20230
  Phone: 202/377-3176

- For a comprehensive review of legislation dealing with lobbying as well as case studies of major lobbying efforts, write for *The Washington Lobby* at:

  The Congressional Quarterly
  1735 K Street, N.W.
  Washington, D.C.   20006

- To find out which attorney has experience in municipal law, contact your Lawyer's Referral Service of the local County Bar Association.

BIBLIOGRAPHY

Should the reader wish to explore this subject more, we recommend the following works, all of which were consulted in preparation of this volume.

Allen, Richard V.; Bartlett, Hall; Colegrove, Kenneth. *Democracy and Communism*. Princeton, N. J.: D. van Nostrand Co., Inc., 1967.

Bennett, James T.; DiLorenzo, Thomas J. *Underground Government: The Off-Budget Public Sector*. Washington, D.C.: Cato Institute, 1983.

Brookes, Warren T., *The Economy in Mind*. New York: Universe Books, 1982.

Brown, Susan Love; Keating, Karl; Mellinger, David; Post, Patrea; Smith, Stuart; Tudor, Catriona. *The Incredible Bread Machine*. San Diego: World Research, Inc., Campus Studies Institute Division, 1978.

Champions of Freedom. Ludwig von Mises Lecture Series. Hillsdale, Mich.: Hillsdale College Press, 1974.

Cornuelle, Richard. *Healing America*. New York: G. P. Putnam's Sons, 1983.

Dale, Duane. *How to Make Citizen Involvement Work: Strategies for Developing Clout*. Citizen Involvement Training Project. Amherst, Mass.: University of Massachusetts, 1978.

Eder, George Jackson. *What's Behind Inflation and How to Beat It*. Englewood Cliffs, N.J.: Prentice-Hall, Inc., 1979.

Edwards, Lee and Anne. *You Can Make the Difference*. New York, Arlington House, 1968.

Fenton, Edwin, editor. *A New History of the United States — An Inquiry*

Approach. Carnegie-Mellon Social Studies Curriculum. New York: Holt Rinehart and Winston, Inc., 1975.

Ferrara, Peter J. *Social Security: Averting the Crisis.* Washington, D.C.: Cato Institute, 1982.

Foner, Eric. *Tom Paine and Revolutionary America.* New York: Oxford University Press, 1976.

Friedman, Milton. *There's No Such Thing as a Free Lunch.* LaSalle, Ill.: Open Court Publishing Co., 1975.

Friedman, Milton and Rose. *Free to Choose.* Harcourt Brace Jovanovich, 1980.

Goodman, John C. *The Regulation of Medical Care: Is the Price Too High?* San Francisco: Cato Institute, 1980.

Greene, Leonard M. *Free Enterprise Without Poverty.* New York: W. W. Norton & Co., 1981.

Hayek, Friederich A. *The Road to Serfdom.* London: Routledge, 1944.

Hazlitt, Henry. *Man Versus the Welfare State.* Lanham, Md.: University Press of America, 1983.

Johnson, Paul. *Modern Times: The World from the Twenties to the Eighties.* New York: Harper & Row, Publishers, 1983.

Kemp, Jack. *An American Renaissance: A Strategy for the 1980s.* New York: Harper & Row, Publishers, 1979.

Kirk, Russell. *The Roots of American Order.* LaSalle, Ill. Open Court Publishing Co., 1975.

Kirk, Russell. *The Conservative Mind.* Sixth Edition. Chicago: Regnery Gateway, 1978.

Kristol, Irving. *Two Cheers for Capitalism.* New York: Basic Books, Inc., Publishers, 1978.

Machlup, Fritz, editor. *Essays on Hayek.* Hillsdale, Mich.: Hillsdale College Press, 1976.

Minot, George Richards. *The History of the Insurrections in Massachusetts in the Year 1786 and the Rebellion Consequent Thereon.* Freeport, N.Y.: Books for Libraries Press. Reprint of 1810 original edition.

Mises, Ludwig von. *Human Action.* Chicago: Contemporary Books, Inc.

Morris, Richard B. *The American Revolution: A Short History.* New York: D. van Nostrand Company, Inc., 1955.

Read, Leonard E. *Vision.* Irving-on-Hudson, N.Y.: The Foundation for Economic Education, Inc., 1978.

Ringer, Robert J. *Restoring the American Dream.* New York: Harper & Row, Publishers, 1979.

Robertson, A. Haeworth. *The Coming Revolution in Social Society.* McLean, Va.: Security Press, Inc. 1981.

Roche, George Charles, III. *The Bewildered Society.* Hillsdale, Mich.: Hillsdale College Press, 1974.

—————. *Education in America.* Hillsdale, Mich.: Hillsdale College Press, 1977.

—————. *Frederic Bastiat, A Man Alone.* Hillsdale, Mich.: Hillsdale College Press, 1977.

—————. *Legacy of Freedom.* Hillsdale, Mich.: Hillsdale College Press, 1969.

Ross, Donald K. *A Public Citizen's Action Manual.* New York: Grossman Publishers, 1973.

Sennholz, Hans F. *Age of Inflation.* Belmont, Mass.: Western Islands Publishing, 1979.

Simon, William E. *A Time for Action.* New York: Reader's Digest/ Berkley Books, 1980.

—————. *A Time for Truth.* New York: Reader's Digest Press, 1978.

Simpson, Dick; Beam, George. *Strategies for Change: How to Make the American Dream Work.* Chicago: The Swallow Press, Inc., 1976.

Smith, Adam. *The Wealth of Nations.* Baltimore: Penguin books, Inc., 1976.

Stewart, Halley Lecture. *The World's Economic Crisis and the Way of Escape.* Freeport, N.Y.: Books for Libraries Press, 1971. Reprint of 1931 edition.

Strausz-Hupe, Robert; Kintner, William R.; Dougherty, James E.; Cottrell, Alvin J. *Protracted Conflict*. New York: Harper & Row Publishers, 1959.

Williams, Lindsey. *The Energy Non Crisis*. San Diego: CLP Publishers, 1980.

Winter, Ralph K. *Government and the Corporation*. Washington, D.C.: American Enterprise Institute, 1978.

INDEX

A

Abel, I. W., 59
Absenteeism, labor, 64–65
Acreage control, 28
Adams, Charles Francis, 155
Adams, John Quincy, 155
Aeroquip Corporation, 63
Affirmative action, 22
Age of Inflation
    (Sennholz), 158
Agency for International
    Development (AID),
    167–171
Agriculture, 135. *See also*
    Acreage control;
    Agriculture, U.S. Dept.
    of; Farmers
Agriculture, U.S. Dept. of,
    28, 29, 96, 113
Aid to Dependent Children
    (ADC), 36, 70, 71, 147
Alabama state employees, 23
Allen, Gary, 204
Ambulance service, 87–88
American Association of
    Poison Control Centers,
    104
American dream, 173
American Federation of
    Labor (AFL), 47
American Hospital
    Association, 102
American Productivity
    Center, 51
Anguiano, Lupe, 68–69, 74
Anti-Americanism and
    foreign aid, 167
Antitrust laws
    enforcement of, 110
    and unions, 56

Apathy, 184
Atomic Energy Commission
    (AEC), 31
Authority, 9. *See also*
    Government, legitimacy
    of; Government, Power
    of; Power
Automation, 135
Automobile industry, 35,
    54–55, 96, 111

B

Bank Credit Analyst, 148
Banking industry
    and controlled interest
        rates, 127
    self-service in, 164
Barter, 127, 203
Basketball, 16–17
Battle of Britain, 177
Bell Laboratories, 36
Black market, 125–126. *See
    also* Cash economy
Blacks, employment among,
    61-63
Bodyguards, government, 29
Bogus, John, 119
Bond market, 121, 123, 124,
    202
Boren, Senator David L.,
    106–108
Boston Tea Party, 119
Bowdoin, Governor James,
    153, 155
Bronx, New York, 88
Buckskins, 119, 121
Budget, federal
    balancing 124, 159–160,
        203

219

and interest on national
    debt, 123
Bureaucracy
    attitudes of, 10
    constituency of, 33
    and delay, 22, 100–101
    errors of, 94
    and job tenure, 27
    and negative income tax
        76, 197
    and news media, 188–190
    power of, 89
    in Social Security
        Administration, 83
    strikes by, 56–58, 196
    and tax reform, 76, 200
    See also Civil Service;
        Government
        personnel; Regulatory
        agencies
Bureau of Engraving,
    120–123
Bureau of Indian Affairs, 110
Butz, Earl, 28
Buying power
    diminished, 202
    increasing, 48,49, 197
    See also Currency; Dollar;
        Inflation

C

Califano, Joseph, 25
California
    and Environmental
        Protection Agency,
        103
    and Truman election, 192
Capital
    formation, 50, 84, 138–140
    investment
        and inflation, 120, 201
        in Japan vs. United
            States, 50
Carter, Jimmy, 99, 173, 207
Cash economy, 127,
    157–158, 203
CB Sports, Inc. 92–93

Central Intelligence Agency
    (CIA), 25, 173
Certificate of need, 20
Chemical industry, 109–110
Child labor laws, 63, 196
Chrysler Corporation, 54
Citibank, 125
Citizen involvement
    and control of
        government, 162–167,
        183–190, 208–209
    and inflation, 180–183
Civil Service
    job security in, 27
    reform, 44–45
    salaries, 25–26
    See also Bureaucracy;
        Government
        personnel
Civil War, 133, 194
Coal
    conversion, 106
    mining, 96, 113–114
Coin-shaving, 116–118
Collective bargaining
    and public employees,
        57–58
    and union monopolies,
        59–60
    See also Labor negotiations;
        Strikes
Colorado, and
    Environmental
    Protection Agency, 103
Common Sense (Paine)
    on abuse of power, 16, 31,
        33, 57, 71, 100, 107,
        149, 151, 183, 185,
        186
    on citizen apathy, 184
    on cooperative effort, 64,
        65
    on ends of government,
        52, 57, 141
    on government debt, 81,
        102, 123, 161
    on government as
        necessary evil, 41, 116
    on independence, 68, 192
    on legislative assembly,

G